INTEGRATED READING AND WRITING

GRADE 3

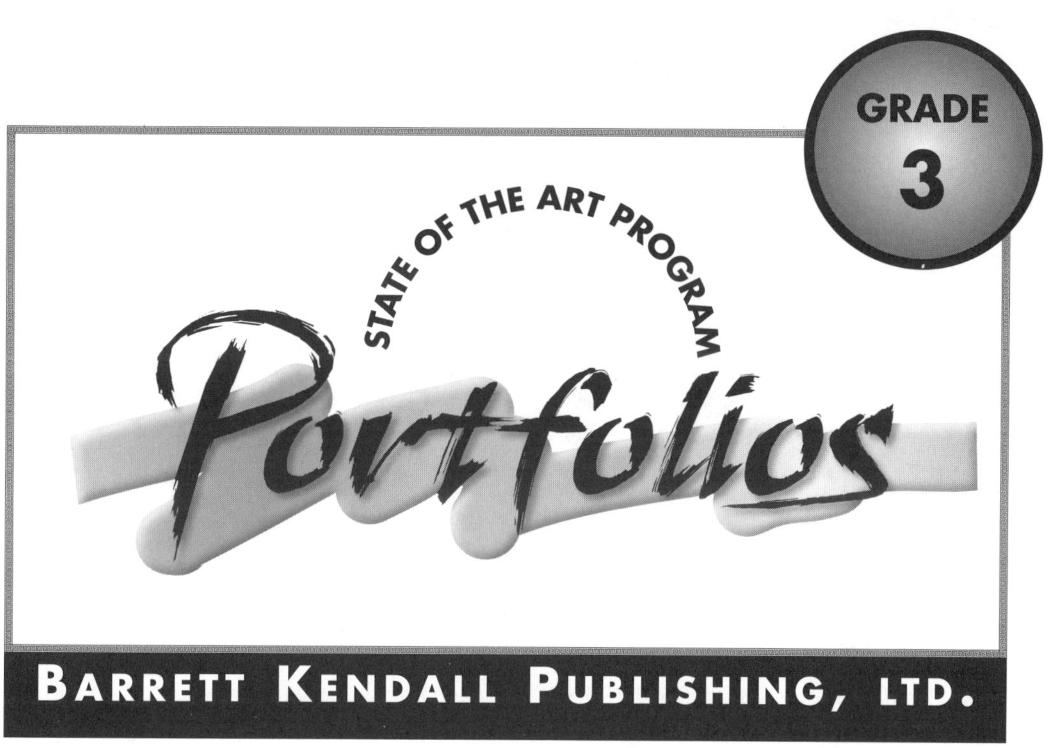

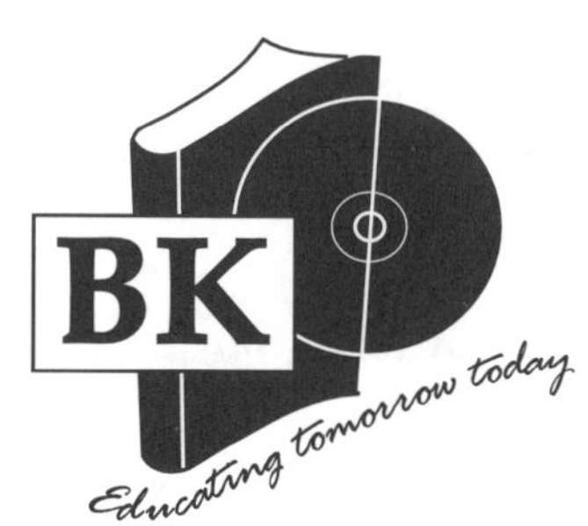

TABLE OF CONTENTS

To the Teacher...

Integrated Reading and Writing gives students an opportunity to prepare for state achievement tests while enriching their understanding of the artworks and art principles presented in the ***Portfolios: State of the Art*** program.

Each of the six units in ***Integrated Reading and Writing*** matches the corresponding unit in ***Portfolios.*** Each lesson corresponds to either the Unit Opener, one of the three lessons, or the end-of-unit material.

Using the Lessons in the Program

Each lesson begins with a lesson planner which organizes the three pages that follow. First, students view the artwork which is the focus of the lesson. Next, they learn the name of the article they will read and review key vocabulary, using the Focus on Words section. Finally, they make predictions about the content of the article. As they do, they explore background knowledge that will help them read the article with understanding.

Each lesson contains a high-interest reading article related to the artwork in the matching ***Portfolios*** unit. The articles are patterned after the kind of reading material found in state achievement tests: informative, narrative, descriptive, and persuasive.

Following the reading, students answer six critical thinking questions based on a standard test format used in state achievement tests.

A writing prompt follows, directing students to write a composition in the descriptive, informative, narrative, or persuasive mode. A graphic organizer is provided to help students generate ideas and organize their thoughts before writing.

Resource Material

Blackline Masters are provided to give students additional assistance with reading and writing, as needed. Two blackline masters (Word Web Making Predictions) assist students who need extra help in reading the articles. Three blackline masters (Venn Diagram and Story Map) help students prepare for the writing activity.

Self-Assessment Masters can be used by students after they have completed their written compositions. These masters allow students to check their compositions to make sure their writing meets the standards you have set.

Word Cards highlight the art-related vocabulary students encounter in the articles. These cards can be used in a variety of ways to enhance learning and increase vocabulary.

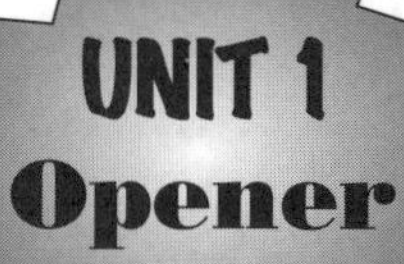

How We Look at the World

SET THE STAGE

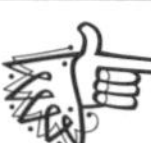

Tell students that they will read an article entitled *How We Look at the World*. Then, use the Focus on Words section on this page to help them make predictions. You may wish to write the words on the chalkboard.

FOCUS ON WORDS

gallery   microscope

magnifying glass   organisms

telescope

Make Predictions

RESOURCE:
TRANSPARENCY
3-9

Ask students to look at the painting by Seurat, *A Sunday on La Grande Jatte-1884* (TRANSPARENCY 3-9). What is unusual about this painting? Have students think about the words as you read the title of the article. Encourage them to predict how each word could be used in an article about how we look at the world. Use the activity as a springboard to access what they already know about things we use to look at our world. (Example: A <u>magnifying glass</u> helps us see tiny things. It makes them seem larger.)

Read

Have students read the article on page 6. After they complete the first two paragraphs, pause. Make sure students understand what is meant by a "flea's-eye view" of the world. Ask students to make predictions about what the rest of the article will be about. Then, have them complete the article.

Respond

Help students complete the questions on page 7. (See Answer Key, page 125.) Then lead them through the reading of the writing prompt on page 8. Discuss the subject they are to write about, the mode of writing, and the audience they will be addressing. Make sure they know how to use the graphic organizer to generate ideas for their written responses.

How We Look at the World

Imagine that you are in an art gallery, standing several feet away from Georges Seurat's *A Sunday on La Grande Jatte.* You see a big scene. You see people, sunlight and shadow, water and trees. You clearly see umbrellas, a dog, and toy boats on the pond. Imagine that you move much closer to see the details in the painting. Now you see the dots of light and color that Seurat used to create each shape.

Can you imagine what it might be like to get an even closer look at nearby things? What does the world look like to a flea, jumping around in that black dog's fur? To get a flea's-eye view of the world, you could use a magnifying glass. Your flea's-eye view would be even more detailed than Seurat's! Each of the dog's hairs would look thick and bushy, like a tree in a forest in which the flea is wandering. If you had a microscope, you could see tiny nearby things even more clearly. For example, you could look at a drop of water from the river Seine and see tiny organisms moving around in it.

Now suppose you want to look at the details of something huge and far away, like the moon. Through a telescope you can see moon valleys and moon mountains and moon colors. If your telescope is very, very powerful, you can see details of planets, and even details of solar systems many millions of miles away from Earth.

Scientists are not the only ones who want to see the world clearly. Artists do, too. Imagine that Georges Seurat was using a microscope and a telescope at La Grand Jatte. What things might he be able to show that are even tinier than his dots? As night falls and people go home, what might Seurat be able to show that is even larger than the park?

Choose the best answer.

1. What is the main idea of the first paragraph?

   ○ **A** how a painting looks from two different distances

   ○ **B** having fun at a park on a Sunday afternoon

   ○ **C** how to paint pictures of dogs and boats

   ○ **D** why you should use dots when you paint

2. What do scientists do with microscopes and magnifying glasses?

   ○ **A** see how fleas view the world

   ○ **B** test powerful instruments

   ○ **C** view very small things

   ○ **D** look at things that are far away

3. In the second paragraph, the word *organisms* means

   ○ **A** musical instruments.

   ○ **B** living things.

   ○ **C** drops of water.

   ○ **D** tools for scientists.

4. How are microscopes and telescopes alike?

   ○ **A** They are the same size.

   ○ **B** They are used by most artists.

   ○ **C** They both cost a great deal of money.

   ○ **D** They both show details.

5. According to this article, artists and scientists are alike because

   ○ **A** they show their work in art galleries.

   ○ **B** they want to see the universe clearly.

   ○ **C** they make pictures of mountains and valleys.

   ○ **D** they look at people in parks.

6. According to the last paragraph, Seurat might use a telescope

   ○ **A** to show details of the moon over the park.

   ○ **B** to show people going home.

   ○ **C** to paint a picture of a scientist.

   ○ **D** to make a dot painting of the lake.

Write a Fantasy Story

Plan and Write Imagine that you and a group of others journeyed to another planet. Write a fantasy story for your classmates about what happens when you arrive. Be sure to name the planet and give your reasons for going there.

Use the story map below to plan your paragraphs. Then, write your story on another sheet of paper.

Name your characters. Tell where and when the story takes place. Write a beginning sentence that grabs your readers attention.

Characters: **Planet and Time:**

Beginning Sentence (reason why you are there):

What problem do the characters have? Tell about it in a sentence.

Problem:

Tell what happens to the characters and what they do.

First Event:

Second Event:

Third Event:

How does the story end? Tell how the problem is solved.

Solution:

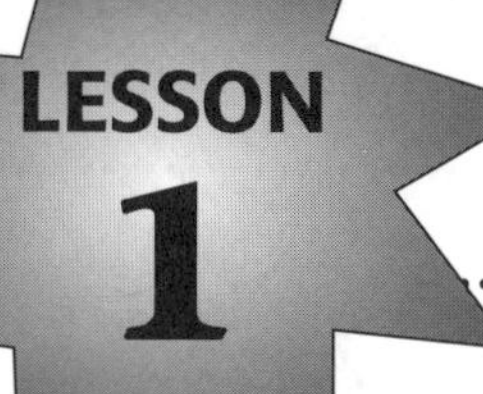

Happy Holidays!

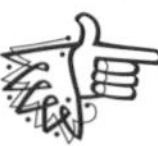

SET THE STAGE

Tell students that they will read an article entitled *Happy Holidays!* Then, use the Focus on Words section on this page to help them make predictions. You may wish to write the words on the chalkboard.

FOCUS ON WORDS

originally	**significance**
universal	**international**

Make Predictions

RESOURCE:
Transparencies
3-1, 3-2

Ask students to look at the two paintings from this lesson, Alma Gunter's *Dinner on Grounds* and Miguel Vivancos' *Village Feast* (TRANSPARENCIES 3-1, 3-2). In what ways are these paintings about holidays? Have students think about the words as you read the title of the article. Encourage them to predict how each word could be used in an article about holidays. Use the activity as a springboard to access what they already know about holidays and how they are celebrated. (Examples: Some holidays, like New Year's Day, are <u>international</u>, celebrated throughout the world. The Fourth of July is a holiday that has great <u>significance</u> for Americans.)

Read

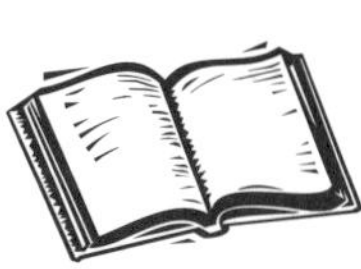

Have students read the article on page 10. After they complete the first paragraph, pause. Ask them to look again at *Dinner on Grounds* and *Village Feast* and discuss the differences in the two kinds of holidays they depict. Ask students to read on and learn more about holidays.

Respond

Help students complete the questions on page 11. (See Answer Key, page 125.) Then lead them through the reading of the writing prompt on page 12. Discuss the subject they are to write about, the mode of writing, and the audience they will be addressing. Make sure they know how to use the graphic organizer to generate ideas for their written responses.

Integrated Reading and Writing: Grade 3

Happy Holidays!

What pops into your mind when you see the word *holiday*? Maybe it's a day you celebrate with a special group. That's the kind of holiday shown in the painting *Dinner on Grounds*, where members of a church are gathered together for a picnic. Sometimes the word *holiday* may make you think of a day when your whole community celebrates together. That's the kind of holiday you see represented in the painting *Village Feast*.

The word *holiday* originally meant *holy day*. Around the world, many holidays today are still religious celebrations. Examples are Passover, Christmas, Posada, and Divali. Another group of holidays honors events or people of great significance in a country's history. For example, in the United States, Americans celebrate the Fourth of July, Martin Luther King Day, and Veterans Day. In Ghana, the Ga people have a month-long festival called Homowo. This celebration began a long time ago when a huge harvest saved the people from dying of starvation.

Some holidays are universal. All over the world, people celebrate traditional holidays like New Year's Eve, and newer ones like Earth Day. For young people, there is International Children's Book Day on April 2nd. This holiday celebrates Hans Christian Andersen's birthday and his contributions to children's stories. Children retell their favorite stories, share book news with pen pals from different countries, and draw illustrations about their favorite books.

It would take a long, long time to list all the holidays in the world. Just think! While you're reading this, there are probably several holidays being celebrated somewhere in the world.

Choose the best answer.

1. According to this article, Martin Luther King Day is a
   - ○ **A** religious holiday.
   - ○ **B** United States holiday.
   - ○ **C** worldwide holiday.
   - ○ **D** holiday in August.

2. In the second paragraph, the word *originally* means
   - ○ **A** new and different.
   - ○ **B** never.
   - ○ **C** in a church.
   - ○ **D** at first.

3. According to the first paragraph, the word *holiday*
   - ○ **A** brings different ideas to our minds.
   - ○ **B** is usually connected to food.
   - ○ **C** reminds us of our nation's history.
   - ○ **D** tells about a special group.

4. What is something else kids might do on International Children's Book Day?
   - ○ **A** clean up their rooms
   - ○ **B** write letters to authors
   - ○ **C** travel to other countries
   - ○ **D** interview Hans Christian Andersen

5. How are Homowo and the Fourth of July alike?
   - ○ **A** They both celebrate a time in history.
   - ○ **B** They both last for a whole month.
   - ○ **C** They both happen in the same month.
   - ○ **D** They both celebrate a big harvest.

6. Another good title for this article is
   - ○ **A** How To Count Holidays.
   - ○ **B** Different Names for Holidays.
   - ○ **C** Holidays Around the World.
   - ○ **D** How To Get Ready for a Holiday.

Write an Informative Paragraph

Plan and Write Think of a holiday you enjoy. It might be a national holiday, or it might be a special celebration your family has. Write a paragraph to a friend describing the holiday. Use the chart below to plan your paragraph. Then, write your paragraph on another sheet of paper.

Begin with a sentence that tells what the holiday is called, when the holiday takes place, and who celebrates it.

Beginning Sentence:

List three details about the holiday. Your details should tell the reader about special things people do, either on the day of the holiday, or preparing for it.

First Detail:

Second Detail:

Third Detail:

Write an ending sentence that tells why the holiday is special to you.

Ending Sentence:

LESSON 2

Different Kinds of Games

SET THE STAGE

Tell students that they will read an article entitled *Different Kinds of Games*. Then, use the Focus on Words section on this page to help them make predictions. You may wish to write the words on the chalkboard.

FOCUS ON WORDS

team sport   **center of interest**

motion

make-believe games

Make Predictions

RESOURCE:
TRANSPARENCIES
3-2, 3-3

Ask students to look at the paintings *The Football Players* by Henri Rousseau and *Children's Games* by Pieter Brueghel the Elder (TRANSPARENCIES 3-2, 3-3). What are these paintings about? What did the painters do to make the paintings interesting? Have students think about the words as you read the title of the article again. Encourage them to predict how the words could be used in an article about different kinds of games. Use the activity as a springboard to access what they already know about playing games. (Examples: When we pretend to be a character, or when we make our toys act out stories, we are playing make-believe games. When we play baseball or hockey, we are playing a team sport.)

Read

Have students read the article on page 14. After they complete the first three paragraphs, pause to ask questions about the different kinds of games discussed. Before beginning paragraph four, ask students to look again at the two paintings for this lesson.Then, ask students to complete the article.

Respond

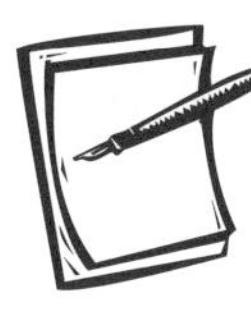

Help students complete the questions on page 15. (See Answer Key, page 125.) Then lead them through the reading of the writing prompt on page 16. Discuss the subject they are to write about, the mode of writing, and the audience they will be addressing. Make sure they know how to use the graphic organizer to generate ideas for their written responses.

Integrated Reading and Writing: Grade 3

Different Kinds of Games

All of us love to play games! If you are by yourself, you may play a game on your computer. You might shoot baskets all alone on a playground or in your driveway. You still feel the need to make points and have fun.

How about games in which one person plays against one or more other people? Examples are hopscotch, checkers, and chess. Other games include tennis, racing, and ice-skating, and wrestling, weight lifting, and swimming contests. In these games, your goal is to shine as the super star who can beat out the other player or players.

In the painting *Children's Games*, you can see games that a person may play alone, like rolling a hoop. You can also see games that are played with others, like jacks or marbles. If you look closely, you can also find a team sport that looks a lot like baseball. You can see another example of a team sport in the painting *The Football Players*.

In *The Football Players*, the ball is the center of interest. The artist places it just out of reach. He shows the player's foot off the ground, stretching his hands upward to catch the ball. This gives the viewer a feeling of action. We feel much the same thrill and sense of fun that we feel when we actually play a team sport.

Other kinds of games are fun, too. In make-believe games, you and your friends might pretend to be grown-ups, or super heroes and villains in stories you like. You could act out a story that you know, or make one up as you go along. You might use your toys to help you.

Games don't end when childhood ends. Look at the adults in *Children's Games* and *The Football Players*. You, too, will enjoy games of all kinds as you get older.

Choose the best answer.

1. Which of the following would be a good title for the fifth paragraph?
   - ○ **A** Pretending to be a Grown-Up
   - ○ **B** Playing Games of Make-Believe
   - ○ **C** Games for Lots of People
   - ○ **D** Playing With Toys

2. In the fourth paragraph, the phrase *center of interest* means
   - ○ **A** of special importance.
   - ○ **B** the feeling of motion.
   - ○ **C** a kind of game.
   - ○ **D** a special color.

3. According to this article, most adults
   - ○ **A** play team games.
   - ○ **B** like crossword puzzle, and chess.
   - ○ **C** enjoy games of all kinds.
   - ○ **D** like to watch their children play games.

4. In *Children's Games* and *The Football Players*, you see
   - ○ **A** games played long ago.
   - ○ **B** hints for winning at team sports.
   - ○ **C** games of make-believe.
   - ○ **D** games people still play today.

5. Which of the following is an OPINION expressed in the passage?
   - ○ **A** All of us love to play games.
   - ○ **B** *Children's Games* shows people playing alone.
   - ○ **C** The center of interest in *The Football Players* is the football.
   - ○ **D** A person can play a computer game alone.

6. After looking at *The Football Players*, you can predict that the next thing that will happen is
   - ○ **A** the players will win the game.
   - ○ **B** the team will call for "time out".
   - ○ **C** the player will catch the ball.
   - ○ **D** the ball will go over the fence.

Write a How-to Paragraph

Plan and Write Think about your favorite game. It may be a game you play by yourself. It may be a game you play against another player, or a game in which you are a member of a team.

Write a paragraph telling a friend how to play the game. Use the chart below to plan your paragraph. Then, write the paragraph on another sheet of paper.

Write a topic sentence that tells the name of the game and the goal or purpose of the game.

> **Topic Sentence:**

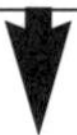

Tell how to play the game. Tell the steps in order, using time-order words such as *first, next,* and *then.*

> **First Step:**
>
> **Second Step:**
>
> **Third Step:**

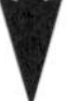

Tell why the game is fun for you.

> **Ending Sentence:**

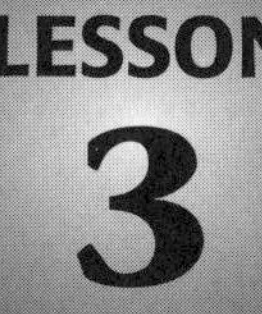

LESSON 3

Lovable Pigs

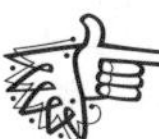
SET THE STAGE

Tell students that they will read an article entitled *Lovable Pigs*. Then, use the Focus on Words section on this page to help them make predictions. You may wish to write the words on the chalkboard.

FOCUS ON WORDS

reputation	talents	expression
texture	outwits	

Make Predictions

RESOURCE:
TRANSPARENCY
3-5

Ask students to look at the painting by James Wyeth, *Portrait of Pig* (TRANSPARENCY 3-5). What kind of pig did the artist paint? What did the artist do to make the painting interesting? Have students think about the words as you read the title of the article. Encourage students to predict how each word could be used in an article about a pig. Use the activity as a springboard to access what they already know about pigs. (Example: The texture of a pig's ears is soft and silky.)

Read

Have students read the article on page 18. After they complete the first paragraph, pause to ask questions about the reputation most pigs have. Before beginning the rest of the article, ask students to recall the pigs in *Charlotte's Web* and the movie *Babe*. Were these pigs different from their reputation? Ask students to complete the article.

Respond

Help students complete the critical thinking questions on page 19. (See Answer Key, page 125.) Then lead them through the reading of the writing prompt on page 20. Discuss the subject they are to write about, the mode of writing, and the audience they will be addressing. Make sure they know how to use the graphic organizer to generate ideas for their written responses.

Lovable Pigs

In some ways, pigs have a bad reputation. For example, we have sayings like "fat as a pig," "eats like a pig," "dirty as a pig," and "lazy as a pig." In Andrew Wyeth's *Portrait of Pig*, however, the pig looks warm and cuddly. Perhaps that is because the artist put real texture into the painting. The hundreds of short lines representing the pig's hair and the hay make us feel like reaching out and touching the painting. What expression do you see on this pig's face? This expression may remind you of stories in which pigs are lovable, smart, and funny.

The first pig story many people hear is a rhyme that makes a baby giggle, as grown-ups wiggle the baby's toes. The rhyme begins "This little piggy went to market. . . ." That's not a lazy pig at all! The next pig story you may remember is "The Three Little Pigs." In this story the third pig is clever. He outwits the wolf by building a house so strong that the wolf can't blow it down.

A famous storybook pig is Wilbur in *Charlotte's Web*. Most readers like Wilbur right away because he is full of interesting questions. He is hopeful about his future, too, and kind and friendly to everyone. Like Charlotte the spider, readers want Wilbur to live a long and happy life.

Babe, in the movie of that name, is certainly not a lazy pig. In fact, he makes the effort to become a sheepherder, like his dog friends. Viewers are delighted when Babe finally succeeds and proves that pigs have many talents.

In real life, the Vietnamese pot-bellied pig is a popular pet. These pigs are easily housebroken, smart enough to learn many commands, like to snuggle, and become devoted to their owners.

Perhaps we should change those sayings about pigs. Maybe we should say "smart as a pig," "lovable as a pig," and "hard-working as a pig."

Choose the best answer.

1. The word *texture* in this article means
   - A colors that are soft and warm.
   - B a high-pitched sound.
   - C something you want to touch.
   - D an appealing animal.

2. The name of the pig in *Charlotte's Web* is
   - A Andrew.
   - B Wilbur.
   - C Babe.
   - D Little Pig.

3. If you choose a pot-bellied pig, you will probably have
   - A a warm and obedient pet.
   - B a pet that is slow and lazy.
   - C a pet that can herd sheep.
   - D a pet that cannot be trained.

4. The word *outwits* in this passage means
   - A loves the outdoors.
   - B tells jokes.
   - C runs away.
   - D thinks better.

5. This passage is mostly about
   - A pig stories for babies.
   - B famous movie pigs.
   - C pigs as pets.
   - D the reputation of pigs.

6. Babe, Wilbur, and the third little pig are alike because
   - A they all live on farms.
   - B they all fool other animals or people.
   - C they all have qualities we admire.
   - D they all appear in portraits of pigs.

Write a Comparison

Plan and Write Think about animals that have certain reputations. What kind of reputation does a fox, snake, pig, cat, sheep, or turtle have? Choose one of these animals as your make-believe pet.

Write three short paragraphs for your classmates telling how you feel about your pet. Use the Venn diagram below to plan your paragraphs. Then, write your paragraphs on another sheet of paper.

Having a Make-Believe Pet

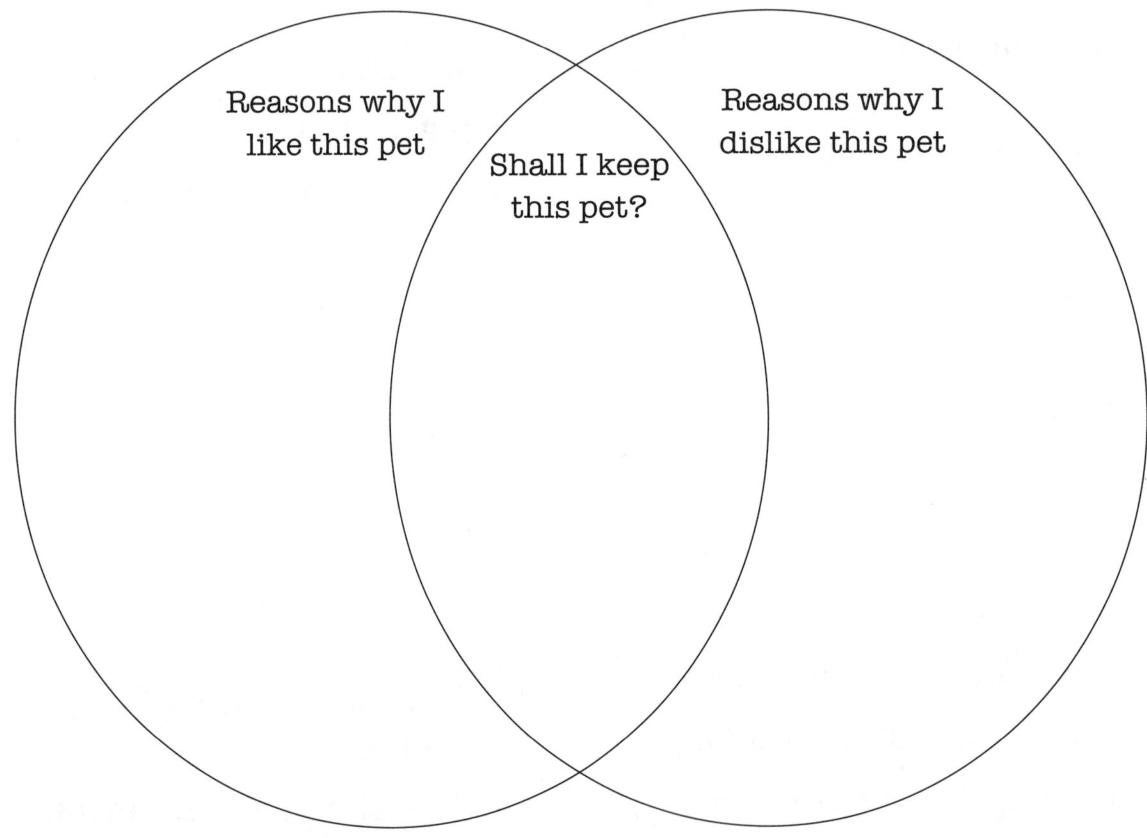

Tips for Writing a Comparison

1. Begin the first paragraph with a topic sentence that tells about your pet. Give two or three details that tell why you like your pet.

2. Begin the second paragraph with a topic sentence, too. Then give two or three details that tell why you dislike your pet.

3. Write a conclusion. Tell why or why not you would keep this creature as a pet.

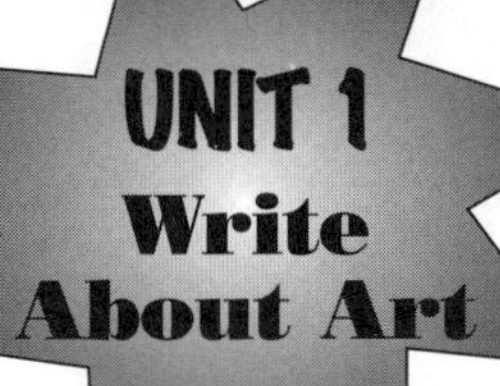

Journeys

SET THE STAGE

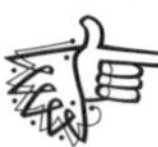

Tell students that they will read an article entitled *Journeys*. Then, use the Focus on Words section on this page to help them make predictions. You may wish to write the words on the chalkboard.

FOCUS ON WORDS

destination   goal

unlike   challenge

Make Predictions

RESOURCE:
TRANSPARENCY
3-11

Ask students to look at the painting by Paul Klee called *Park near Lu(cerne)* (TRANPARENCY 3-11). How is this painting like a map? Have students think about the words as you read the title of the article again. Encourage them to predict how each word could be used in an article about journeys or travel. Use the activity as a springboard to access what they already know about travelling. (Examples: Going somewhere without getting lost can be a <u>challenge</u>. Our <u>goal</u> is to reach our <u>destination</u> by dinner time.)

Read

Have students read the article on page 22. After they complete the first three paragraphs, pause. Make sure students understand how maps and mazes are alike and how they are different. Ask students to make predictions about what the rest of the article will be about. Then, have them complete the article.

Respond

Help students complete the questions on page 23. (See Answer Key, page 125.) Then lead them through the reading of the writing prompt on page 24. Discuss the subject they are to write about, the mode of writing, and the audience they will be addressing. Make sure they know how to use the graphic organizer to generate ideas for their written responses.

JOURNEYS

Meet Lena! She loves finding new places. However, she can't always really travel, so she takes a lot of make-believe trips. Pictures, maps, and mazes help Lena on her imaginary journeys. And no matter how she travels, Lena always knows her goal, or destination.

One way Lena travels is with mazes. In these fun games, the player has to draw a line from <u>Start</u> to a big goal somewhere in the maze. For a mouse, the goal may be a slice of cheese. For a pirate, the goal may be a treasure chest. The pathways twist and turn and most of them end up in deadends. Only one pathway leads to the goal.

Lena also uses maps for her imaginary trips. She imagines going from her home in Brooklyn, New York, to faraway places like Fairbanks, Alaska; Paris, France; or New Delhi, India. With a world map, Lena gets a bird's-eye view of the world. She can see many, many different routes she might take from her home to her make-believe destination.

One day Lena saw a picture that was like both a maze and a map! The picture was Paul Klee's *Park near Lu(cerne)*. The destination seemed to be the tree at the center of the picture. Lines leading to the tree reminded Lena of the lines in a maze. However, unlike a maze, there were many ways of reaching the goal. In that way, the picture was like a map. The traveler could start anyplace, and still end up at that tree!

Now Lena wants to take on the challenge of making her own map-maze-picture. She wants to show just one destination, but many ways of getting there. She wants the traveler to see the goal, and to enjoy the trip in her or his own way.

Choose the best answer.

1. Which statement is true about Lena?

   ○ **A** She travels all over the world.
   ○ **B** She is moving from New York to France.
   ○ **C** She is drawing a picture of a park.
   ○ **D** She has a great imagination.

2. In this story, what does *goal* mean?

   ○ **A** a score you make in a game
   ○ **B** a destination you want to reach
   ○ **C** a pathway you follow
   ○ **D** a treasure chest filled with coins

3. To Lena, how are maps and mazes alike?

   ○ **A** They are both too hard to use.
   ○ **B** They both lead to just one place.
   ○ **C** They are both puzzles.
   ○ **D** They both show paths from one place to another.

4. Why does *Park near Lu(cerne)* interest Lena?

   ○ **A** The picture looks like both a maze and a map.
   ○ **B** The picture shows a park near her home.
   ○ **C** The picture was painted by Paul Klee.
   ○ **D** The tree is one that Lena has climbed.

5. Another good title for this story is

   ○ **A** How to Make Maps and Mazes.
   ○ **B** Lena's Unusual Journeys.
   ○ **C** A Park near Lu(cerne).
   ○ **D** Lena's Report Card.

6. What is Lena now going to try to draw?

   ○ **A** a picture that is a maze and a map
   ○ **B** a picture just like Paul Klee's
   ○ **C** a picture that shows many destinations
   ○ **D** a picture that shows just one way to go

Name____ Date_______________ Class____________

Write a Comparison and Contrast Composition

Plan and Write Paul Klee chose a special place as the subject of *Park near Lu(cerne)*. What places are special to you?

Choose two places to compare and contrast. Write a composition for your teacher about them. Use the chart below to plan your composition. Then, write it on a another sheet of paper.

Write a sentence that names the two places. Then, write two sentences that tell how the places are alike.

First Paragraph:

Write three sentences that tell what is special and different about the first place.

Second Paragraph:

Write three sentences that tell what is special and different about the second place.

Third Paragraph:

Write a concluding sentence that tells why both places are important to you.

Fourth Paragraph:

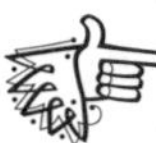

Dreams of a Village

Tell students that they will read an article entitled *Dreams of a Village*. Then, use the Focus on Words section on this page to help them make predictions. You may wish to write the words on the chalkboard.

FOCUS ON WORDS

images	curious
overlap	primary colors
imagination	

Make Predictions

RESOURCE:
TRANSPARENCY
3-18

Ask students to look at the painting *I and the Village*, by Marc Chagall (TRANSPARENCY 3-18). What is this painting about? What makes the painting unusual? Have students think about the words as you read the title of the article again. Encourage them to predict how each word could be used in an article about painting and dreams. Use the activity as a springboard to access what they know already about dreams. (Example: A dream is a picture made by your <u>imagination</u>.)

Read

Have students read the article on page 26. After they complete the first two paragraphs, pause and let students look again at Chagall's painting. Have volunteers point out the animal, the milkmaid, and the village. Before beginning paragraph three, ask students to share what they know about the reasons why we dream. Then, ask students to complete the article.

Respond

Help students complete the critical thinking questions on page 27. (See Answer Key, page 125.) Then, lead them through the reading of the writing prompt on page 28. Discuss the subject they are to write about, the mode of writing, and the audience they are to address. Make sure they know how to use the graphic organizer to generate ideas for their written responses.

Dreams of a Village

The painting *I and the Village* shows the place where Marc Chagall grew up. In the center of the picture, a woman is milking a cow. In the distance, there is a church. Nearby, you can see the houses of the town.

Does this painting show a real village? The animal head seems to be the center of interest, yet it is too large for the rest of the painting. Curious images are tossed together—some are seen up close, and some are far away. The scene looks and feels like a dream.

When we are awake, our brain is like a hunter running down a path. We think of something, such as a house. Our brain hunts in its memory for a particular house, perhaps the one in which we live. Our brain shows us a clear picture of a house.

However, if we dream of a house, our brain works differently. Now it is like an explorer, but one who is able to try many different paths at the same time. The house we dream of may combine parts of many different buildings. It may have our own bedroom in it. But it may have a staircase we have never seen before, or part of a room in our school.

Chagall's painting shows his brain operating as an explorer. He creates pictures from the past and lets them float in space. They seem to drift, and as they do, they overlap. The large animal head is staring out, as if in a dream. Perhaps the animal is dreaming of the milkmaid. But who is the milkmaid? She may or may not be someone Chagall knew as a child. At the top of the painting, a dream village with its church tower floats into the night. Perhaps this is the village of his childhood.

Chagall believed in the power of the imagination. This painting explores the childhood he felt deeply about. The bright primary colors he chose show the happiness he felt then.

Choose the best answer.

1. When we dream, the author says, our brain is like
- ○ **A** a painter.
- ○ **B** a milkmaid.
- ○ **C** an explorer.
- ○ **D** a hunter.

2. The word *curious* in this article means
- ○ **A** bright.
- ○ **B** important.
- ○ **C** unusual.
- ○ **D** real.

3. Chagall lets his images drift and overlap because
- ○ **A** he is not able to paint any other way.
- ○ **B** he wants to make a modern painting.
- ○ **C** he is using a new style of painting.
- ○ **D** he is showing his memories and his dreams.

4. What is another good title for this article?
- ○ **A** A Country Village
- ○ **B** Dreams of Houses
- ○ **C** An Artist Paints His Dreams
- ○ **D** A Hunter Searches for a House

5. Which of the following is an OPINION of Chagall's painting?
- ○ **A** Compared to the rest of the painting, the animal head is large.
- ○ **B** Toward the center of the painting, a woman is milking a cow.
- ○ **C** At the top of the painting, there is a village.
- ○ **D** Some people think this is Chagall's most beautiful painting.

5. According to this article, Chagall's choice of primary colors shows his feelings of
- ○ **A** happiness.
- ○ **B** sadness.
- ○ **C** grief.
- ○ **D** confusion.

Name_______________________________________ Date_____________ Class____________

Write a Fantasy Story

Plan and Write Think about a memory from your life. Do you remember a favorite pet, or a strange house you once saw? Do you remember a wonderful toy you once owned? Write a fantasy story for your classmates about your memory. Perhaps the toy comes to life, or the pet becomes a hero. Perhaps the strange house is a home for aliens.

Use the story map below to plan your story. Then, write your story on another sheet of paper.

Name your characters. Tell where and when the story takes place.
Write a beginning sentence that will grab your reader's attention.

Characters:	**Where:**
	When:
Beginning Sentence:	

What problem do the characters have? Tell about it in a sentence.

Problem:

One of more of your characters decides to act. Tell what happens.

First Event:

Second Event:

Third Event:

How does the story end? Tell how the problem is solved.

Solution:

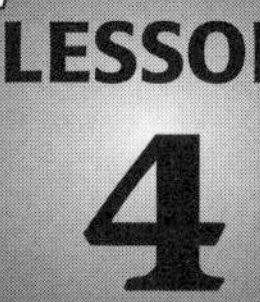

LESSON 4

Colors for a Landscape

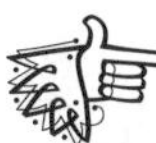

SET THE STAGE

Tell students that they will read an article entitled *Colors for a Landscape*. Then, use the Focus on Words section on this page to help them make predictions. You may wish to write the words on the chalkboard.

FOCUS ON WORDS

hues   **warm colors**

cool colors   **color scheme**

related colors

Make Predictions

RESOURCE:
TRANSPARENCY
3-12

Ask students to look at the painting *The Turning Road*, by André Derain (TRANSPARENCY 3-12) and note the artist's choice of colors. Invite them to consider other colors that might be used in a painting of a landscape. Have students think about the words as you read the title of the article again. Encourage them to predict how each word could be used in an article about colors for a landscape. Use the activity as a springboard to access what they already know about landscapes. (Example: You need to figure out a <u>color</u> <u>scheme</u> when you paint a landscape.)

Read

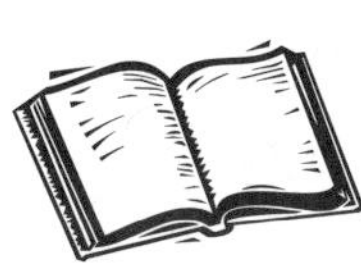

Have students read the article on page 30. After they complete the first two paragraphs, pause to ask questions about the distinction between warm colors and cool colors. Ask students to comment on their own responses to color. Have students continue to read about the color scheme used by Derain.

Respond

Help students to complete the critical thinking questions on page 31. (See Answer Key, page 125.) Then, lead them through the reading of the writing prompt on page 32. Discuss the subject they are to write about, the mode of writing, and the audience they are to address. Make sure they know how to use the graphic organizer to generate ideas for their written responses.

Colors for a Landscape

Warm colors make us think of warm things. Reds, oranges, and yellows remind us of fire and the sun. Warm colors make us think of strong feelings, such as love or excitement. Some people think that warm colors are the colors of life because red is the color of blood. Also, yellow is the color of the sun, and the sun makes life possible.

Cool colors remind us of cool things. Blues and greens make us think of cool water, the sky, and leaves on trees. Violets remind us of sunsets, when the shadows come and the earth cools off. Cool colors help us feel calm and restful.

People respond to warm colors and cool colors differently. Babies look first at objects in bright, warm hues, such as red. Walls in a dentist's office are often painted in cool greens and blues to help patients relax as they wait for their appointments.

If you were painting trees, you would choose browns, blacks, and grays for tree trunks. Look at the painting *The Turning Road* by André Derain. The tree trunks are brilliant and glowing. The artist began with warm reds and yellows. As he painted, he blended these colors with related colors, yellow-orange and red-violet, to create bright, bold trees. Then, he put touches of red on the people. Finally, he painted a golden road in a curve through the whole painting.

The Turning Road is alive with the warm feelings the artist has for his subject. His color scheme helps him share his love for this landscape and the people who live within it.

Choose the best answer.

1. Which of these states a FACT found in the article?

○ **A** The painting gives people a happy feeling.

○ **B** The artist uses too much red and red orange.

○ **C** The color on the trees does not blend.

○ **D** Real tree trunks contain shades of browns, blacks, and grays.

2. According to the article, warm colors remind us of

○ **A** lakes and rivers.

○ **B** ice.

○ **C** leaves on a tree.

○ **D** life itself.

3. What does the word *landscape* mean in this article?

○ **A** an indoor scene

○ **B** an outdoor scene

○ **C** a group of people

○ **D** the sky at night

4. Why would a dentist's office walls be painted in blues and greens?

○ **A** Warm colors make us feel warm.

○ **B** Cool colors help patients relax.

○ **C** Blended colors are attractive.

○ **D** Related colors are soothing.

5. What does the word *hues* mean in this article?

○ **A** landscapes

○ **B** tree trunks

○ **C** colors

○ **D** fruits

6. Derain began painting the tree trunks with red and yellow, then he

○ **A** blended these colors with related colors of yellow-orange and red-violet.

○ **B** selected cool colors for the water.

○ **C** painted a golden road through the painting

○ **D** Added touches of red to the people.

Write a Description

Plan and Write Think of a landscape. It could be a place you visited once, such as a sandy beach or a winding road up a high hill. It might be a photograph or a postcard of a faraway place.

Write a paragraph for your teacher that describes this place. Use the web below to plan your paragraph. Write the name of the landscape in the middle of the chart. Think about what it is like to sense the landscape. What do you see? What do you hear? What do you smell? What can you touch? Write some of these details in the outer ovals of the web. Then, write your paragraph on a separate sheet of paper.

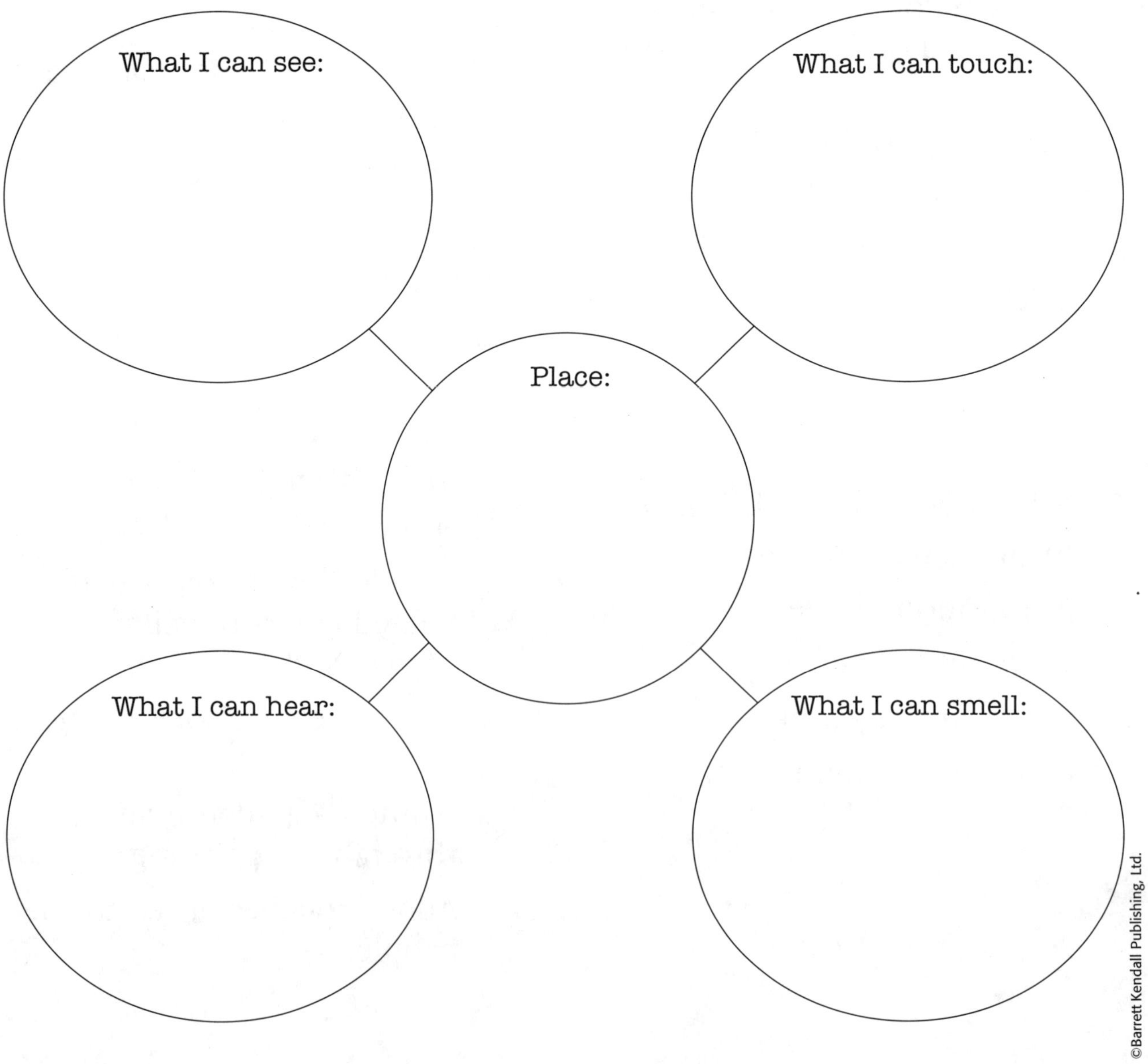

32 **DESCRIPTIVE WRITING: *UNIT 2, LESSON 4***   Integrated Reading and Writing: Grade 3

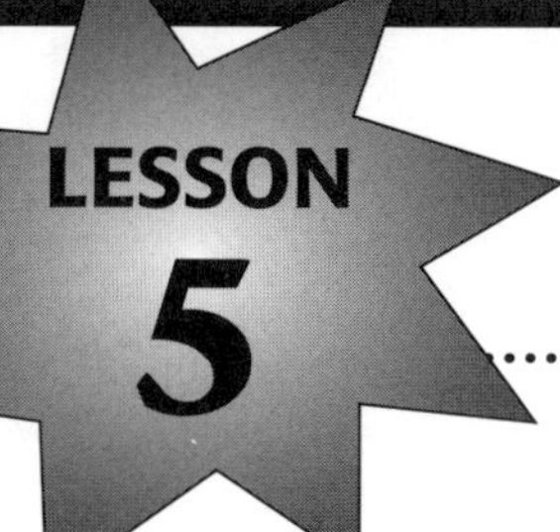

LESSON 5

Honoring the Best

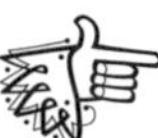

SET THE STAGE

Tell students that they will read an article entitled *Honoring the Best*. Then, use the Focus on Words section on this page to help them make predictions. You may wish to write the words on the chalkboard.

FOCUS ON WORDS

still life   rectangles

tribute   pose

Make Predictions

RESOURCE:
TRANSPARENCIES
3-13, 3-14

Ask students to look at the painting by Pat Steir called *The Brueghel Series* (TRANSPARENCY 3-14). What makes this painting unusual? Have students look at *Blumen in der Nacht* by Gabriele Münter for an example of a still life painting that mimics the styles of artists that she admired (TRANSPARENCY 3-13). Have students think about the words as you read the title of the article. Encourage them to predict how each word could be used in an article about honoring people we admire. Use the activity as a springboard to access what they already know about honoring someone. (Example: When we do something in a public fashion to thank someone, we are paying <u>tribute</u> to that person.)

Read

Have students read the article on page 34. After they complete the first paragraph, pause and let them look at Steir's painting again. Ask a volunteer to point out where the rectangles are. Before beginning paragraph three, ask students to think of other ways we can honor people we admire (celebrate them at a party, award them a prize). Then, ask students to complete the article.

Respond

Help students complete the questions on page 35. (See Answer Key, page 125.) Then lead them through the reading of the writing prompt on page 36. Discuss the subject they are to write about, the mode of writing and, the audience they are to address. Make sure they know how to use the graphic organizer to generate ideas for their written responses.

Honoring the Best

Most of us appreciate our teachers. Pat Steir did, too. Her teachers were great artists such as Rembrandt and Rubens. Their great works helped her understand art. She painted *The Brueghel Series* in their honor. *The Brueghel Series* is a still life depicting a bouquet of flowers in a blue vase made from sixty-four rectangles. Each rectangle is painted in the style of one of a great artist.

People like to pay tribute to those they admire. Many paintings of George Washington, for instance, show him in a glorious light. He looks larger than life and quite noble. Such paintings are a way to show our appreciation and express our gratitude.

Statues are another way that we pay tribute to great women and men. These works of art often show the hero on horseback or in a grand pose. The artist tries to give us a feeling of the dignity and stature of the person.

A state or nation also honors great men and women by setting aside special days for them. On Martin Luther King Day, we honor a man who fought for equal rights. On Memorial Day, we remember the sacrifices of our soldiers. We even set aside special days to honor our parents, Mother's Day and Father's Day.

There are other, less obvious ways of honoring someone. A young person may choose to follow in a parent's footsteps or join the profession of someone he or she admires. By choosing the same profession or living by the same beliefs, the young person is saying, "I not only approve of your life, but I want my life to be like yours." This is perhaps the greatest tribute of all.

Choose the best answer.

1. What feeling does Pat Steir have toward the great artists of the past?
   - **A** anger
   - **B** sadness
   - **C** gratitude
   - **D** peace

2. Which of the following is an example of a still life?
   - **A** a bowl of fruit
   - **B** a galloping horse
   - **C** a few birds flying overhead
   - **D** a group of people talking together

3. What is another good name for this article?
   - **A** Painting in Rectangles
   - **B** Holidays Are for Heroes
   - **C** Honoring George Washington
   - **D** Paying Tribute to People We Admire

4. Another word for *pose* is
   - **A** help.
   - **B** admire.
   - **C** position.
   - **D** noble.

5. According to the article, what is the greatest tribute you can offer to someone you admire?
   - **A** to help them
   - **B** to imitate them
   - **C** to praise them
   - **D** to teach them

6. Why did Pat Steir paint this picture?
   - **A** to win a prize
   - **B** to paint some flowers in her home
   - **C** to honor great artists of the past
   - **D** to show her skill

Name____ Date____________ Class____________

Write a Realistic Story

Plan and Write Think of a person that you admire. Perhaps he or she is a person you know, a person from history, or some other famous person. Think about the qualities of the person that you admire. What are this person's special talents or skills?

Write a character sketch for your teacher in which you describe this person. Use the chart below to plan your work. Then, write your character sketch on another sheet of paper.

Write a topic sentence naming the character you are going to describe.

Topic Sentence:

Add details about how the character looks and acts.

How the Character Looks:

How the Character Acts:

Tell about the character's special talents or skills.

Special Talents or Skills:

Write an ending sentence that summarizes your thoughts about the character and tells why he or she is someone that you admire.

Ending Sentence:

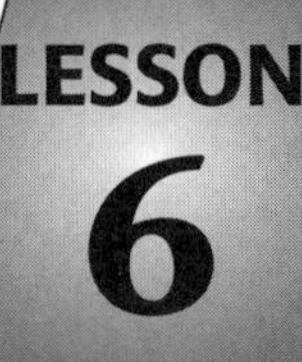

LESSON 6

Animals in Inuit Life

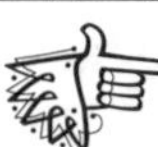

SET THE STAGE

Tell students that they will read an article entitled *Animals in Inuit Life*. Then, use the Focus on Words section on this page to help them make predictions. You may wish to write the words on the chalkboard.

FOCUS ON WORDS

shaman

custom   **myths**

masks   **print**

Make Predictions

RESOURCE:
TRANSPARENCY
3-16

Look at the print by Kenojuak Ashevak called *Young Owl Takes a Ride* (TRANSPARENCY 3-16). What attitude does it suggest? Have students think about the words as you read the title of the article. Encourage students to predict how each word could be used in an article about how the Inuit people feel about animals. Use the activity as a springboard to access what they already know about the Inuit people. (Example: <u>Masks</u> with animal faces might be worn on the faces of the Inuit people.)

Read

Have students read the article on page 38. After they complete the first two paragraphs, pause to ask students to consider what it would be like to depend on animals in the wild for all their needs. Discuss what it means to them to live in harmony with nature. Then, ask students to complete the article.

Respond

Help students complete the questions on page 39. (See Answer Key, page 125.) Then, lead them through the reading of the writing prompt on page 40. Discuss the subject they are to write about, the mode of writing, and the audience they are to address. Make sure they know how to use the graphic organizer to generate ideas for their written responses.

Animals in Inuit Life

Imagine two owls having fun together! That's what you see in the print *Young Owl Takes a Ride.* The young owl is enjoying a piggyback ride with its mother. The picture shows the bond between the baby and its parent. It also shows the sense of humor of the artist, an Inuit named Kenojuak Ashevak.

The Inuit people are Eskimos who live in Canada. Animals are at the center of their lives. Winter lasts ten months where they live, and most of the time it is dark. The people have always depended on sea animals for food, fuel, clothing, tools, and housing. Seals, walruses, and whales are the most important. These animals provide meat, oil, and fur. Even boats are covered with animal skins. Animal bones are used to make knives and needles.

The Inuit do not believe that they are more important than animals. Instead, they believe that all things are connected and depend upon one another. All things have the same right to the earth. The world is united, and spirit can be found in everything, from animals and rocks to humans.

In Inuit myths, the souls of animals and people have deep relationships. The *shaman,* or holy man, is especially close to animal souls and to the greater spirits. He asks the spirits of animals to help the people avoid sickness, bad hunting, and bad weather.

Like many Native American peoples, the Inuit express their admiration and awe for animals in their art and customs. Inuit masks are a way of honoring the spirits of game animals so that the hunt will succeed. The print *Young Owl Takes a Ride* is a way for an Inuit artist to enjoy a joke with an animal friend.

Choose the best answer.

1. Which of the following is a FACT stated in the article?
   ○ **A** The Inuit people are afraid of birds.
   ○ **B** All Inuit people are artists.
   ○ **C** A shaman conducts church services for the Inuits.
   ○ **D** Where the Inuit live, winter usually lasts ten months.

2. What does the word *myths* mean in this article?
   ○ **A** stories
   ○ **B** prayers
   ○ **C** bones
   ○ **D** animals

3. Why do the Inuit people wear masks?
   ○ **A** to participate in community games
   ○ **B** to honor the spirits of game animals
   ○ **C** to honor the spirits of the dead
   ○ **D** to participate in community plays

4. According to the author, what is funny about *Young Owl Takes a Ride*?
   ○ **A** The owl is painted blue.
   ○ **B** A young owl is taking a piggyback ride with its mother.
   ○ **C** The owl has feathers that spread out in all directions.
   ○ **D** The owl is standing on the ground, not flying.

5. According to the article, the most important animals to the Inuits are seals, whales, and
   ○ **A** beavers.
   ○ **B** birds.
   ○ **C** polar bears.
   ○ **D** walruses.

6. What does the word *shaman* mean in this article?
   ○ **A** an owl
   ○ **B** a cry from the spirit world
   ○ **C** a holy man
   ○ **D** an artist

Write About an Animal

Plan and Write Think about an animal that you like. Choose one that is special to you. It may be a pet, a zoo animal, or an animal you have only seen in pictures.

Write a paragraph telling a friend about this animal. Use the chart below to plan your paragraph. Then, write the paragraph on a separate sheet of paper.

Begin with a sentence that will grab your reader's attention.

Beginning Sentence:

Write several sentences that tell about your animal. Describe what it looks, feels, and sounds like.

Looks:

Feels:

Sounds:

Write an ending sentence that tells why this animal is special to you.

Ending Sentence:

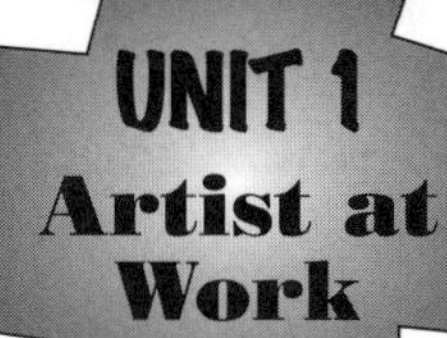

Birthday Beginnings

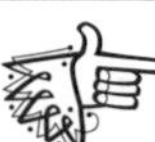 **SET THE STAGE**

Tell students that they will read an article entitled *Birthday Beginnings*. Then, use the Focus on Words section on this page to help them make predictions. You may wish to write the words on the chalkboard.

FOCUS ON WORDS

slanted line   motion

shield   centuries

Make Predictions

RESOURCE:
TRANSPARENCY
3-17

Ask students to look at the painting *Birthday* by Marc Chagall (TRANSPARENCY 3-17). Invite them to discuss their personal impressions of the artwork. Have students think about the words as you read the title of the article again. Ask students to predict how each word could be used in an article about the painting and about birthdays. Although students are not expected to know, use the activity as a springboard to access what they already know about celebrating birthdays. (Example: People have been celebrating their birthdays for <u>centuries</u>.)

Read

Have students read the article on page 42. After they complete the first paragraph, pause to ask questions about the painting. Make sure they see the flowers and understand that the artist is kissing his wife. Have them use a ruler to find the slanted line in the painting. Then, ask students to complete the article.

Respond

Help students to complete the questions on page 43. (See Answer Key, page 125.) Then, lead them through the reading of the writing prompt on page 44. Discuss the subject they are to write about, the mode of writing and, the audience they are to address. Make sure they know how to use the graphic organizer to generate ideas for their written responses.

Birthday Beginnings

It is the birthday of Marc Chagall's wife. The painting *Birthday* shows him giving her flowers. He leans down to kiss her and she reaches up to him. Their two bodies form a slanted line across the picture. This makes them seem to be in motion, floating in the air in pure happiness.

Are you happy on your birthday? Most of us are. We love a birthday party with our friends. We remember family and friends, too, on their birthdays.

Long ago, people believed in spirits, both good and evil. They thought that these spirits came close to a person having a birthday. So friends and relatives gathered around the birthday child. They gave gifts and good wishes to shield her or him from danger. They shared a meal together on the birthday to add to the blessings of good spirits and godmothers. The first birthday parties were supposed to help protect the birthday child from evil and bring goodness to his or her life.

Blowing out candles on birthday cakes is a tradition that began centuries ago, in ancient Greece and Rome. People believed that candles carried prayers and wishes up to the gods. So they began putting candles on birthday cakes. The birthday child made a secret wish. If all the candles were blown out at once, it was believed that the wish might be granted.

Playing games at birthday parties is another tradition. Long ago, games of skill and strength were played to show how much the birthday child had learned. Friends and family were proud to see the child's improvement each year. They joined with the child to celebrate the old year and the beginning of a new year.

Choose the best answer.

1. What is the subject of Chagall's painting?
   - ○ **A** a game of sport and skill
   - ○ **B** spirits of good and evil
   - ○ **C** magical candles
   - ○ **D** the artist and his wife

2. What did Chagall use to create motion in his painting?
   - ○ **A** color
   - ○ **B** shapes
   - ○ **C** line
   - ○ **D** texture

3. The word *centuries* in this article means
   - ○ **A** old ideas.
   - ○ **B** serious thoughts.
   - ○ **C** hundreds of years.
   - ○ **D** happy times.

4. In the beginning, why did people have birthday parties?
   - ○ **A** to honor the person
   - ○ **B** to say goodbye
   - ○ **C** to protect the person
   - ○ **D** to check the person's skill

5. When did people start putting candles on birthday cakes?
   - ○ **A** hundreds of years ago
   - ○ **B** about a hundred years ago
   - ○ **C** a few years ago
   - ○ **D** about fifty years ago

6. The word *shield* in this article means
   - ○ **A** a metal object.
   - ○ **B** to protect.
   - ○ **C** to fight.
   - ○ **D** a badge.

Write a Realistic Story

Plan and Write Think of a birthday party that you really enjoyed. Perhaps it was your own birthday party, or that of someone else. Write a realistic story for your classmates about what happened. Use the chart below to plan your story. Then, write your story on another sheet of paper.

Name the characters in your party story. Tell where and when the story takes place. Write a beginning sentence that will grab your reader's attention.

Characters:	**Where:**
	When:
Beginning Sentence:	

What problem do the characters have at the party? Tell about it in a sentence.

Problem:

Tell what happens to each character and what they do.

First Event:

Second Event:

Third Event:

How does the story end? Tell how the problem is solved.

Solution:

A Wedding Sculpture

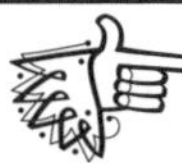

UNIT 3 Opener

👉 SET THE STAGE

Tell students that they will read an article entitled *A Wedding Sculpture*. Then, use the Focus on Words section on this page to help them make predictions. You may wish to write the words on the chalkboard.

FOCUS ON WORDS

sculpture

found object

assemblage

symbol

formal

Make Predictions

RESOURCE:
TRANSPARENCY
3-28

Show the transparency of Louise Nevelson's *Dawn's Wedding Chapel* (TRANSPARENCY 3-28). Ask students what is unusual about the artwork. Have students think about the words as you read the title of the article. Encourage them to predict how each word might be used in an article about a sculpture for a wedding. Use the activity as a springboard to access what they already know about weddings. (Possible student responses: A wedding is a <u>formal</u> activity. A wedding ring is a <u>symbol</u> of marriage.)

Read

Have students read the article on page 46. After they complete the first paragraph, pause. Invite them to read the second and third paragraphs with their books open to the picture of *Dawn's Wedding Chapel*. Tell them that the second and third paragraphs refer to different parts of the structure. They will need to refer to the picture as they complete the article.

Respond

Help students complete the critical thinking questions on page 47. (See Answer Key, page 126.) Then, lead them through the reading of the writing prompt on page 48. Discuss the subject they are to write about, the mode of writing, and the audience they are to address. Make sure they know how to use the graphic organizer to generate ideas for their written responses.

A Wedding Sculpture

When Louise Nevelson decided to create a sculpture, she chose a different way to create its form. Instead of chipping at a piece of stone to create a form, she began searching for pieces of wood. She gathered small pieces and large pieces wherever she could find them. Because she found these pieces, we call them found objects.

Nevelson built her sculpture by sorting and choosing these found objects, based on size and shape. Then, she arranged them inside boxes. She filled seven boxes and stacked them, one upon another. The entire structure stands 7 1/2 feet high. She then painted it white and called it *Dawn's Wedding Chapel.*

Look at the picture of her sculpture. First you see straight lines—on the outside edges and within the boxes. When you look again, you see round forms. Some are curves and curls. One corner looks like a carving for a table. Another edge looks like a piece of lace. As you look, you begin to see why Nevelson called her beautiful white structure a "wedding chapel."

Nevelson painted her assemblage white because brides wear white. The color white is a symbol for purity. Nevelson called her sculpture a chapel because weddings often take place in a chapel, or some sacred place. A wedding is usually a formal ceremony, based on old customs. For example, the bride wears a veil, a custom that dates back about 2,000 years. The bride and groom exchange rings. The wedding ring is a circle and a symbol of eternal love, since a circle has no beginning and no end.

Like a wedding gown, Louise Nevelson's sculpture is formal, all-white, and pleasing to the eye. And, like a wedding ceremony, it is carefully planned and filled with important details. Louise Nevelson seems to have picked the perfect title for her sculpture.

Choose the best answer. Fill in the circle next to your choice.

1. According to the first paragraph, a sculpture is an art piece that has
   - ○ **A** form.
   - ○ **B** sound.
   - ○ **C** color.
   - ○ **D** line.

2. Which of these is a FACT from the article?
   - ○ **A** A wedding is a beautiful ceremony.
   - ○ **B** Louise Nevelson's sculpture looks like a real chapel.
   - ○ **C** Louise Nevelson made her sculpture from found objects.
   - ○ **D** *Dawn's Wedding Chapel* is a beautiful sculpture.

3. The color white is a symbol of
   - ○ **A** a chapel.
   - ○ **B** eternity.
   - ○ **C** the heart.
   - ○ **D** purity.

4. Another word or phrase for *assemblage* is
   - ○ **A** symbol.
   - ○ **B** structure.
   - ○ **C** found objects.
   - ○ **D** color.

5. How old is the custom of wearing a wedding veil?
   - ○ **A** about one hundred years
   - ○ **B** about thirty years
   - ○ **C** about two thousand years
   - ○ **D** about five hundred years

6. What is a symbol for eternity at a wedding?
   - ○ **A** the color white
   - ○ **B** the ring
   - ○ **C** the bridal veil
   - ○ **D** the wedding gown

Name____ Date_______________ Class_______________

Write About an Object

Plan and Write The wedding ring is very special to a bride and groom. Think about an object that is special to you. It might be a a watch or a chain or a picture.

Write a paragraph telling a friend about this special object. Use the chart below to plan your paragraph. Then, write your paragraph on a another sheet of paper.

Begin with a sentence that grabs your reader's attention.

> **Beginning Sentence:**

Write several sentences that tell about the object. Describe what it looks like, what it does, and what it is used for.

> **What It Looks Like:**
>
> **What It Does or Is Used For:**

Tell where you got the object and where you keep it.

> **How I Got It:**
>
> **Where I Keep It:**

Tell why the object is special to you.

> **Ending Sentence:**

LESSON 7

The Forms in Which We Live

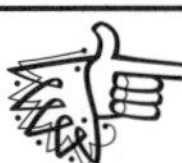

SET THE STAGE

Tell students that they will read an article entitled *The Forms in Which We Live*. Then, use the Focus on Words section on this page to help them make predictions. You may wish to write the words on the chalkboard.

FOCUS ON WORDS

sphere   cube

cylinder   cone

pyramid

Make Predictions

RESOURCE:
PUPIL EDITION
P. 47

Have students think about the words as you read the title of the article. Encourage them to predict how these words could be used in an article about the forms (the structures) in which people live. Use the activity as a springboard to access what they already know about the different shapes of homes. (Possible student responses: The homes on my street are mostly formed like a <u>cube</u>. Some American Indian families lived in teepees, tents shaped like <u>cones</u>.)

Read

Have students read the article on page 50. After they complete the first two paragraphs, pause and let them look back at the pictures of basic forms on page 47 in the student textbook. Ask a volunteer to point out the sphere and explain what the author means by saying an igloo is one half of a sphere. Before beginning paragraph three, remind students to refer to the other forms as they complete the article.

Respond

Help students complete the critical thinking questions on page 51. (See Answer Key, page 126.) Then, lead them through the reading of the writing prompt on page 52. Discuss the subject they are to write about, the mode of writing, and the audience they are to address. Make sure they know how to use the graphic organizer to generate ideas for their written responses.

The Forms in Which We Live

Have you noticed the forms of buildings in your neighborhood? On your way to school, you may pass cubes, rectangles, or perhaps cylinders. These forms have even sizes and certain shapes. They take up space. They are our houses and apartments.

Some of the forms people live in are amazing. For example, think of an igloo.It is one half of a sphere. The Inuit builds an igloo by cutting blocks of snow with a knife. A tunnel entrance, placed away from the wind, keeps cold air out. A skylight made of freshwater ice lets in the light.

Certain American Indian tribes lived in teepees. A teepee is shaped like a cone. The people set poles in the ground in the form of a circle. Then they tilted the poles so that they leaned together at the top. The structure was then covered with deerskin or buffalo hide. It had an opening at the top to let smoke out. The "door" was a flap of hide that could be lifted and lowered.

In the Middle East, you might see a variety of forms—pyramids, cubes, and cones. In earlier times, the people of the Middle East lived wandering lives. They needed homes they could fold up and carry, so they built tents made of wood and cloth. They set up poles arranged in rows, and covered them with felt.

Pioneers built large cubes called log cabins. A log cabin is built along straight lines, but has a gable shaped like a triangle at the top. The gable fills in the space from the wall to the tip of the pointed roof. It forms a protected space, shaped like a pyramid. This space forms an attic where the children slept.

A home is, first of all, a shelter. In some ways, however, a home is also a sculpture. Like the artists Siva and Guanyin, the person building a home chooses a form that reflects a way of life.

Choose the best answer.

1. Which form is most like a American Indian teepee?

   ○ **A** a cylinder

   ○ **B** a cube

   ○ **C** a cone

   ○ **D** a sphere

2. What does the word *shelter* mean in this article?

   ○ **A** a neighborhood

   ○ **B** a place to live

   ○ **C** a round form

   ○ **D** a sculpture

3. Which of these steps is the first thing to do to build a teepee?

   ○ **A** set poles in a circle in the ground

   ○ **B** set an opening in the top for smoke

   ○ **C** lean the poles together at the top

   ○ **D** cover the poles with deerskin or buffalo hide

4. According to the article, why did people of the Middle East build tents they could fold up?

   ○ **A** They needed an escape from their enemies.

   ○ **B** They wanted to provide for newcomers.

   ○ **C** They were a wandering people.

   ○ **D** Tents offer protection from desert heat.

5. Why does a log cabin have a gable on top shaped like a triangle?

   ○ **A** It keeps the house warm.

   ○ **B** It forms an attic where children can sleep.

   ○ **C** It lets in light.

   ○ **D** It reflects the family's way of life.

6. Which of the following is shaped most like a sphere?

   ○ **A** a ball

   ○ **B** a telephone book

   ○ **C** an ice cube

   ○ **D** an ear of corn

Write a How-to Paragraph

Plan and Write In this lesson you learned the steps for making a teepee and an igloo. Think about something you can make or do. Perhaps you know how to cook something. Perhaps you know a craft. Perhaps you know a dance step. Write directions for your teacher about how to do it. Use the chart below to plan your paragraph. Then, write your paragraph on another sheet of paper.

Write your topic. List all the materials you need to perform the activity.

How-to Topic:	**Materials Needed:**

Write a topic sentence that tells what you will be explaining.

Topic Sentence:

Tell about each step. Use time-order words such as *first, next,* and *then*.

First Step:

Second Step:

Third Step:

Tell about the last thing you do. Use time-order words such as *finally* or *last*.

Last Step:

LESSON 8

Pinocchio Becomes Real

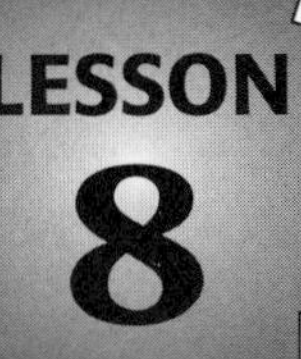

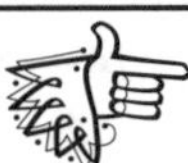

SET THE STAGE

Tell students that they will read an article entitled *Pinocchio Becomes Real*. Then, use the Focus on Words section on this page to help them make predictions. You may wish to write the words on the chalkboard.

FOCUS ON WORDS

asymmetrical balance

rascal   **admit**

misfortune   **puppet**

Make Predictions

RESOURCE:
TRANSPARENCY
3-24

Show the transparency of Alberto Giocometti's *Nose* (TRANSPARENCY 3-24). Ask students to give their reactions to it. Have students think about the words as you read the title of the article. Encourage them to predict how these words could be used in an article about Pinocchio. Use the activity as a springboard to access what they already know about Pinocchio. (Possible student responses: The nose on the sculpture has <u>asymmetrical balance</u>. Pinocchio had to learn to <u>admit</u> that he had been wrong.)

Read

Have students read the article on page 54. After they complete the first two paragraphs, pause and let them talk about puppets. Ask whether or not Pinocchio had strings. (No, he did not.) Point out that ordinarily a puppet is guided by strings, but Pinocchio is free to do as he likes. Then, ask students to complete the article.

Respond

Help students complete the critical thinking questions on page 55. (See Answer Key, page 126.) Then, lead them through the reading of the writing prompt on page 56. Discuss the subject they are to write about, the mode of writing, and the audience they are to address. Make sure they know how to use the graphic organizer to generate ideas for their written responses.

Pinocchio Becomes Real

The figure in *Nose* has an impossible nose! It is much too long for its face! Alberto Giacometti used asymmetrical balance to create the sculpture. The result is a figure that looks like *Pinocchio*. Do you remember that story?

Gepetto, a lonely toy maker, wishes he had a son. One day he carves a boy puppet out of wood and calls it Pinocchio. Before going to sleep that night, Gepetto wishes on a star. He asks that Pinocchio become a real live boy.

The star grants his wish. Pinocchio becomes a boy, but he is still made of wood. A good fairy tells him he must show that he is brave, unselfish, and able to tell right from wrong. When he can do these things, he will become a real live boy.

Trouble is waiting for Pinocchio. First, however, he makes friends with a rascal who promises to make him a star of the theater but sells him to a puppet show instead. Then, he runs off with some boys to Pleasure Island, but he and the boys are turned into donkeys.

When Pinocchio gets into trouble, the fairy visits him and asks him what happened. Pinocchio doesn't want to admit his mistakes. He tells a lie, and all at once, his nose grows longer! When he lies again, his nose grows even longer! When at last he tells the truth, his nose shrinks, and he is freed from his troubled situation.

After all his adventures, the wooden boy manages to do a brave, unselfish thing. He rescues Gepetto, who has been swallowed by a whale. The fairy, who is pleased that Pinocchio has done the right thing, turns him into real live boy. His misfortunes as a puppet are over! The dearest wish of the toy maker and his puppet has come true.

Choose the best answer. Fill in the circle next to your choice.

1. What wish did Geppeto make before he went to sleep?

- ○ **A** that he would have a son
- ○ **B** that he could make another puppet
- ○ **C** that his puppet would become a real boy
- ○ **D** that a good child would buy his puppet

2. What happened to Pinocchio when he told a lie?

- ○ **A** His nose grew.
- ○ **B** He turned to wood.
- ○ **C** The fairy appeared.
- ○ **D** His nose disappeared.

3. How did the fairy feel when Pinocchio told the truth?

- ○ **A** angry
- ○ **B** happy
- ○ **C** sad
- ○ **D** disturbed

4. What does the word *rascal* mean in this article?

- ○ **A** a young child
- ○ **B** a giant
- ○ **C** a man
- ○ **D** a troublemaker

5. What happens to Pinocchio just before he is turned into a donkey?

- ○ **A** He is sold to a puppet show.
- ○ **B** His nose grows very long.
- ○ **C** He rescues his father from the whale.
- ○ **D** He goes to Pleasure Island.

6. What does the word *misfortune* mean in this article?

- ○ **A** bad luck
- ○ **B** youth
- ○ **C** bad dreams
- ○ **D** journey

Write a Fantasy Story

Plan and Write Write a fantasy for a friend in which something impossible happens to the main character. This causes a problem that the character must solve. Use the story map below to help you plan your story. Then, write your story on another sheet of paper.

Name your characters. Tell where and when the story takes place.
Write a beginning sentence that grabs your reader's attention.

Characters:	**Where:** **When:**

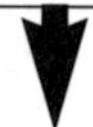

What problem is caused when the impossible happens? (For example, what if the main character is turned into a tree?)

Problem:

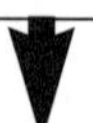

What happens when the character tries to solve the problem?
Make the problem get worse and worse.

First Event:

Second Event:

Third Event:

How does the story end? Tell how the problem is solved.

Solution:

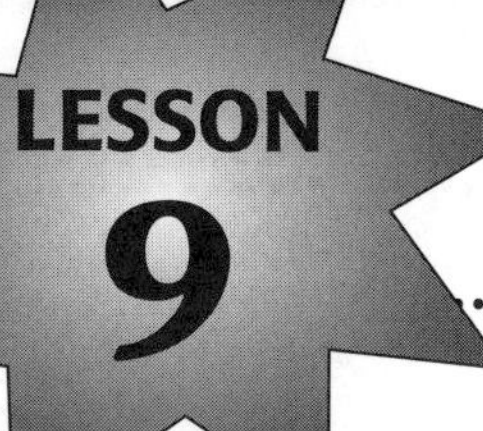

LESSON 9

Silence That Speaks

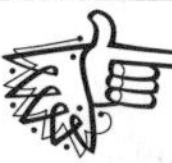

SET THE STAGE

Tell students that they will read an article entitled *Silence That Speaks*. Then, use the Focus on Words section on this page to help them make predictions. You may wish to write the words on the chalkboard.

FOCUS ON WORDS

mute   exterior

vertical lines   subject

mime

Make Predictions

RESOURCE:
TRANSPARENCY
3-26

Show the transparency of *Walk, Don't Walk*. (TRANSPARENCY 3-26). Ask students to decide whether this sculpture would be suitable for their downtown area. Have students think about the words as you read the title of the article. Encourage them to predict how each word could be used in an article about silence and the sculpture *Walk, Don't Walk* by George Segal. Use the activity as a springboard to access what they know about mimes and sculptures. (Possible student responses: A sculpture that is tall may have <u>vertical lines</u>. A <u>mime</u> is an actor who never speaks.)

Read

Have students read the article on page 58. After they complete the first two paragraphs, pause. Discuss the feelings one gets when standing next to someone who is silent. Ask students to continue reading to learn about another art form that relies on silence.

Respond

Help students complete the critical thinking questions on page 59. (See Answer Key, page 126.) Then, lead them through the reading of the writing prompt on page 60. Discuss the subject they are to write about, the mode of writing, and the audience they are to address. Make sure they know how to use the graphic organizer to generate ideas for their written responses.

Silence That Speaks

The artwork named *Walk, Don't Walk* shows life-size people standing together, forming vertical lines on the platform. Vertical lines often create a still, quiet mood. Because these people look so real, we almost think they are real!; however, there is a difference—these people are silent. No one makes a sound. No one shuffles a foot or coughs. No individual turns to look at something. They all stand there in complete silence, forever.

Segal's *Walk, Don't Walk* has some things in common with another art form called mime. It is a soundless art form. Have you ever seen a mime perform?

The actor stands alone on a stage with her or his face painted white. The mime expresses emotions, reveals character, and tells stories in complete silence. Like the figures in the sculpture, the performer creates human drama out of silence. Mime depends on form, just as sculpture does. Mime also uses the body and the face to express feelings and thoughts.

Part of the reason the art of mime makes us think and feel is because it is expressive. Gestures are exaggerated, made larger than life. This helps us see that the performer represents all people. That is the reason mime has been a popular form of art for thousands of years. Its silence allows the audience to focus on the lone performer. The artist can then touch our hearts or our funny bones.

We see ourselves in mime and in sculptures such as Segal's *Walk, Don't Walk*. These artworks help us think about who we are.

Choose the best answer. Fill in the circle next to your choice.

1. The art form called *mime* is performed by
   - ○ **A** a chorus.
   - ○ **B** a single person.
   - ○ **C** animals.
   - ○ **D** three silent people.

2. What does the word *mute* mean in this article?
   - ○ **A** interior
   - ○ **B** loud
   - ○ **C** silent
   - ○ **D** dead

3. Segal's sculpture consists of
   - ○ **A** a performing mime.
   - ○ **B** burlap bags.
   - ○ **C** old cars.
   - ○ **D** three lifelike statues.

4. Which of these states a FACT found in the article?
   - ○ **A** Performers of mime always wear white.
   - ○ **B** Mime is performed to music.
   - ○ **C** Segal, the artist, once performed mime.
   - ○ **D** Mime is an art form that is performed in silence.

5. The word *exterior* is the opposite of the word
   - ○ **A** interior.
   - ○ **B** exaggerated.
   - ○ **C** ordinary.
   - ○ **D** expressive.

6. The vertical lines formed by the three figures and the pole in the artwork create a (an) _____ mood.
   - ○ **A** unsteady
   - ○ **B** busy
   - ○ **C** quiet
   - ○ **D** noisy

Name____ Date____________ Class____________

Write a Friendly Letter

Plan and Write Think of a time when you were surprised because you saw something where you least expected it—a car on top of a store, for example. Write a letter to a friend telling about what you saw. Use the chart below to plan your letter. Then, write your letter on another sheet of paper.

Write the heading and greeting here.

Greeting:	**Heading:** Your address: Today's date:

Dear___________________,
(Write pen pal or the name of the person you are writing to.)

Tell your friend why you are writing the letter. Show your strong feeling about what you saw in the sentence.

Describe what you were doing and where you were when you saw the surprising thing.

First Paragraph:

Describe the surprising thing you saw. If it was an action, explain what happened first, second, and so on, in order. If it is an object, give details about how it looked.

Second Paragraph:

Tell your friend why you wanted to share this story with him or her.

Ending Sentence:

Write the closing in this space.

Closing:
Your friend,

________________________________ (Write your signature here.)

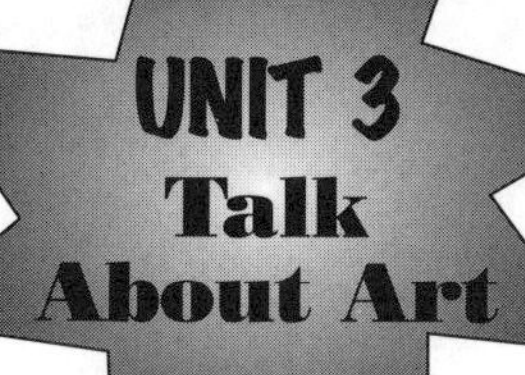

Dear Diary

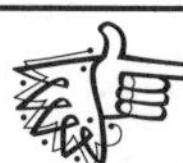

SET THE STAGE

Tell students that they will read an article called *Dear Diary*. Then, use the Focus on Words section on this page to help them make predictions. You may wish to write the words on the chalkboard.

FOCUS ON WORDS

stopper   creek

balance   variety

Make Predictions

RESOURCE:
TRANSPARENCY
3-29

Display the transparency of *Tarot* by Nancy Graves. (TRANSPARENCY 3-29). Explain that this is a large sculpture made of found objects. Ask: What objects do you recognize on this sculpture? Have students think about the words as you read the title of the article. Encourage them to predict how each word could be used in an article based on diary entries from a young person spending her summer on a farm. Use the activity as a springboard to access what they already know about farms. (Possible student response: A <u>creek</u> is a small stream.)

Read

Have students read the article on page 62. After they complete the first two paragraphs, pause. Ask students to describe any pretty things they've found on summer vacations (rocks, shells, etc.). Ask students to continue reading to find out what this young person did with the objects she found.

Respond

Help students complete the critical thinking questions on page 63. (See Answer Key, page 126.) Then, lead them through the reading of the writing prompt on page 64. Discuss the subject they are to write about, the mode of writing, and the audience they are to address. Make sure they know how to use the graphic organizer to generate ideas for their written responses.

Dear Diary

June 24   Dear Diary, I am spending a month on Great-grandpa Joe's farm. We get up early while it is cool. We walk out to the fields to check on the cattle. Today, I found a sky blue egg shell and a feather. Grandpa said they both came from a robin's nest. They were beautiful. I took them back to my room.

July 2   Dear Diary, Grandpa and I went fishing at the creek. Guess what I found! A tiny blue bottle with a glass stopper. It was almost buried in the mud along the bank of the creek. Grandpa said it came from an old farmhouse, probably. People used to get medicine in bottles like this. I took it back to my room. Cleaned up, it looks magical!

July 11   Dear Diary, Yuck! When we got back from our hike today, my socks were full of big, fuzzy burrs. They were hard to get out. They pulled the threads out of my socks. I stacked them next to the shell and the medicine bottle. Up close, they look like monster porcupine-insects.

July 19   Dear Diary, today I found the coolest thing of all—a snake skin. It is smooth and dry with a diamond pattern. Grandpa said that snakes shed their skin as they grow.

I have a great idea! I will make a sculpture from these found objects, like the *Tarot* sculpture. I will get a pretty tree branch and sink it into a big piece of clay. This will be the "stand" for my sculpture. Then I will arrange my found objects on this stand.

I need to think of ways to create a nice balance of objects. I need to think of color, too. Perhaps I should paint the branch or the burrs. I need to create variety, so I may need to find more objects. Oh, this is fun! This will be a great thing to take home to show my friends.

Choose the best answer. Fill in the circle next to your choice.

1. The balance in an artwork refers to
   - ○ **A** the center of interest.
   - ○ **B** the arrangement of the parts.
   - ○ **C** the flow of color.
   - ○ **D** the kind of line used.

2. How did the snake skin get on the ground?
   - ○ **A** An animal killed the snake and left the skin.
   - ○ **B** The snake grew too big for its skin and shed it.
   - ○ **C** Someone put the snake skin out as a trap for other snakes.
   - ○ **D** A snake died and all that is left is its skin.

3. What did the writer use to make her artwork?
   - ○ **A** jewels
   - ○ **B** paints
   - ○ **C** wildflowers
   - ○ **D** found objects

4. When did the author find a shell and a feather?
   - ○ **A** early in the day
   - ○ **B** at noon
   - ○ **C** late in the day
   - ○ **D** at nigh

5. Which of the following will be the "stand" for the sculpture?
   - ○ **A** feather
   - ○ **B** a tree branch
   - ○ **C** a bottle
   - ○ **D** a snake

6. An artwork has variety when
   - ○ **A** the lines are clear and crisp.
   - ○ **B** the color scheme is bright.
   - ○ **C** there are many different things to look at.
   - ○ **D** the texture is easy to see.

Compare and Contrast Old and New Objects

Plan and Write Think of something old that belongs to you. Now think of a way you would like to change it into something new. For example, you could stuff an old sock and make it a puppet. Write a paper for your teacher telling how the old and new objects are alike and how they are different. Use the Venn diagram and tips below to plan your paragraphs. Then, write your paragraphs on another sheet of paper.

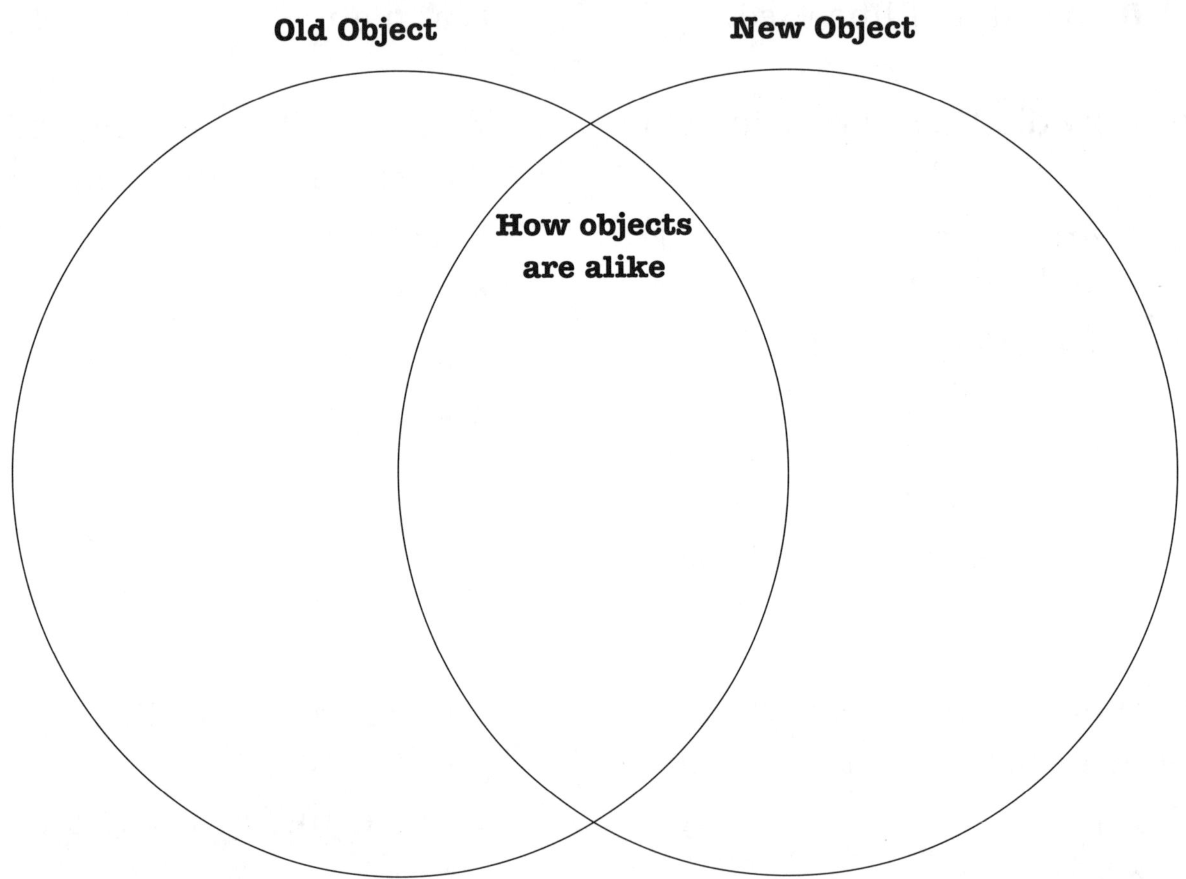

Tips for Comparing

1. Begin the first paragraph with a topic sentence that tells what you are comparing. Give two or three details that tell how the objects are alike.

2. Begin the second paragraph with a topic sentence, too. Then give two or three details that tell how the two items are different.

3. Use signal words such as *both* and *neither*.

4. Write a conclusion. Tell which item you like best and why.

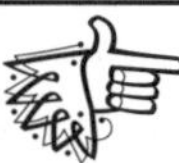

UNIT 4 Opener

Clothing of Long Ago

SET THE STAGE

Tell students that they will read an article entitled *Clothing of Long Ago*. Then, use the Focus on Words section on this page to help them make predictions. You may wish to write the words on the chalkboard.

FOCUS ON WORDS

wealthy   contrast

portrayed   gems

farthingale

Make Predictions

RESOURCE:
TRANSPARENCY
3-39

Show the transparency of the painting *The Chess Game* (TRANSPARENCY 3-39). Ask: What is this painting about? What are the girls doing? Have students think about the words as you read the title of the article. Encourage them to predict how each word could be used in an article about the clothing people wore long ago. Use the activity as a springboard to access what they already know about the Renaissance and the clothing people wore during that time. (Possible student response: By studying their clothing, you can conclude that these girls came from <u>wealthy</u> families.)

Read

Have students read the article on page 66. After they complete the first three paragraphs, pause. Discuss how long ago the Renaissance was. (It was about 500 years ago. Europeans had just discovered America!) Ask students to complete the article and find out how people dressed at this time.

Respond

Help students complete the critical thinking questions on page 67. (See Answer Key, page 126.) Then, lead them through the reading of the writing prompt on page 68. Discuss the subject they are to write about, the writing mode, and the audience they are to address. Make sure they know how to use the graphic organizer to generate ideas for their written responses.

Clothing of Long Ago

The *Chess Game*, painted by Sofonisba Anguissola, shows a teenage girl and her sister playing a game of chess. Do they look like girls you might see today, playing a game in their back yard? No. And, somehow, the two girls don't look young. Why is that?

The girls were painted long ago. They are wearing the rich and colorful clothing of the Renaissance. Anguissola's painting faithfully portrayed the details and shapes she saw. The clothes these girls wear show some things about the way people lived during the Renaissance.

During this time, the individual was important. It was important, therefore, for people to take great care in their dress. They wanted to look as perfect as possible. Clothes were one way of showing pride and joy in being human.

The inside clothing fit the body, as ours does today. However, the outer clothing was padded and puffed and draped in a way that seemed to change the shape of the body. For example, a girl's skirt made her look wider. A hoop skirt called a farthingale was worn under the dress. It had a number of round hoops made of wire or wicker and was shaped like a drum. The outer skirt draped over it and fell straight to the ground. The wide skirt formed a sharp contrast to the girl's small waistline.

The most popular fabrics were dark silk or velvet. This rich material made gold and jewels stand out. People showed how wealthy they were by the gems sewn on their clothing. Look carefully at the rich fabrics the girls in the painting are wearing. Do you see the gold thread woven through the clothing? Do you see the gold braid that outlines the neck and shoulders? The fabric shines in the light, with the soft blue forming a pleasant contrast to the rich red.

Anguissola chose her subjects from real life. By painting with such careful detail, the artist has left us an illustrated history of the way girls dressed more than four hundred years ago.

Choose the best answer. Fill in the circle next to your choice.

1. Which of the following is a FACT stated in the article?

   ○ **A** During the Renaissance, silks and velvets were popular fabrics.

   ○ **B** The girls in the portrait are servants for the king.

   ○ **C** Anguissola painted this portrait in the early 1900's.

   ○ **D** During the Renaissance, clothing was not important.

2. What does the word *gems* mean in this article?

   ○ **A** clothing

   ○ **B** games

   ○ **C** jewels

   ○ **D** animals

3. In what way are these girls different from young girls today?

   ○ **A** They enjoy playing board games, like chess, with each other.

   ○ **B** They like to play outdoors.

   ○ **C** They enjoy wearing beautiful clothing.

   ○ **D** They wear hoops underneath their clothing.

4. According to the article, outer clothing was NOT

   ○ **A** made of silk or velvet.

   ○ **B** designed to show the shape of the body.

   ○ **C** brightly colored.

   ○ **D** trimmed with gold and jewels.

5. People of the Renaissance paid attention to their clothing because

   ○ **A** they had great wealth.

   ○ **B** they wanted to look as perfect as possible.

   ○ **C** beautiful clothing was similar to a piece of art.

   ○ **D** it was difficult to get work without beautiful clothes.

6. What does the word *farthingale* mean in this article?

   ○ **A** a game

   ○ **B** a jewel

   ○ **C** a fabric

   ○ **D** a hoop

Write about Clothing

Plan and Write In *The Chess Game*, the clothes make each girl look special. Do you have an outfit that makes you feel special? Think of your favorite outfit. Write a paragraph for a friend that tells about your outfit and how it makes you feel. Use the chart below to plan your paragraph. Then, write your paragraph on another sheet of paper.

First, write a beginning sentence that tells your reader what clothes you are writing about. Make your beginning sentence as interesting as possible.

Beginning Sentence:

Next, write the body of your paragraph. Explain what your outfit is like. Give details that describe its colors, patterns, shapes, and how it feels.

Colors:

Patterns and shapes:

How it feels:

What people say to me about my outfit:

Write an ending sentence telling how wearing this outfit makes you feel inside.

Ending Sentence:

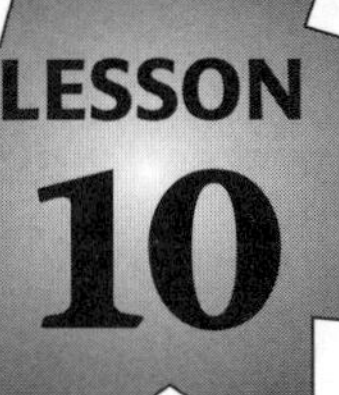

LESSON 10

Caring for New Puppies

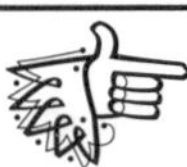

SET THE STAGE

Tell students that they will read an article entitled *Caring for New Puppies*. Then, use the Focus on Words section on this page to help them make predictions. You may wish to write the words on the chalkboard.

FOCUS ON WORDS

squirmy   plump

roly-poly   blended

Make Predictions

RESOURCE:
TRANSPARENCIES
3-32, 3-33

Show the transparencies of Hung Lui's *Feeding the Rabbit* and Lois Mailou Jones' *Mére du Senegal* (TRANSPARENCIES 3-32 and 3-33). Ask: How are the children caring for the rabbit? How is the mother taking care of the child? Have students think about the words as you read the title of the article. Encourage them to predict how each word could be used in an article about caring for new puppies. Use the activity as a springboard to access what they already know about a new puppy. (Possible student response: A new puppy is probably <u>plump</u> and <u>squirmy</u>.)

Read

Have students read the article on page 70. After they complete the first three paragraphs, pause. Discuss what they have learned so far. What will they probably read about in the rest of the article? Ask students to make predictions and then complete the article.

Respond

Help students complete the critical thinking questions on page 71. (See Answer Key, page 126.) Then lead them through the reading of the writing prompt on page 72. Discuss the subject they are to write about, the mode of writing, and the audience they are to address. Make sure they know how to use the graphic organizer to generate ideas for their written responses.

Caring for New Puppies

I could not wait for Rosie to have her puppies. It would be so much fun to play with them! Would they have curly white and brown hair and droopy ears, like Rosie? Would they have her short stump of tail that wagged so fast?

Then, one night, they were born. She had three, then two more. They were tiny and pink and white, like mice. Their eyes were squeezed shut. Rosie began to lick the puppies, but then she whined and lay back down. There were more puppies! I didn't find out until the next morning that Rosie had fifteen puppies! As tiny as they were, they filled up the box.

We knew we would have to help Rosie feed them. So we warmed a special milk. We used an eye dropper to feed each pup. I loved to hold a squirmy body in one hand, wrapped in a soft washcloth to keep it warm. The pups soon learned to suck the milk from the eye dropper. Their jaws were strong!

Soon they were plump, but they still didn't have much fur. It took several weeks before they opened their eyes and began to walk. They were so roly-poly, it made us laugh to see them playing with each other. Now their den was a huge refrigerator box, but they still filled it up.

As they grew, we still helped them eat. We gave them big pans of milk blended with canned food. They would stick their noses in too far and sneeze. Then, they would begin to lap up their dinner. As they did, they walked forward, and soon they were eating their way across the pan! When one reached the other side and stepped out, her brothers and sisters would begin to clean her off.

Now the puppies have soft white and brown fur. Each one has an individual size and shape and personality. Each one is special to me, like a friend.

Choose the best answer. Fill in the circle next to your choice.

1. What did the speaker find out the next morning?
   - ○ **A** Rosie was very ill.
   - ○ **B** Two puppies had run away.
   - ○ **C** Rosie had fifteen puppies.
   - ○ **D** His or her parents would sell the puppies.

2. Why did the family feed the puppies with warm milk?
   - ○ **A** to give the puppies extra vitamins
   - ○ **B** to help Rosie feed the puppies
   - ○ **C** to help the puppies get to sleep
   - ○ **D** to provide something warm for the puppies to eat

3. How long did it take for the puppies to open their eyes?
   - ○ **A** ten days
   - ○ **B** the week-end
   - ○ **C** several weeks
   - ○ **D** one week

4. What does the word *plump* mean?
   - ○ **A** well-rounded
   - ○ **B** thin
   - ○ **C** tall
   - ○ **D** hard and firm

5. How did the puppies eat the milk blended with canned food?
   - ○ **A** by sucking on an eye dropper
   - ○ **B** by sniffing it through their noses
   - ○ **C** by eating their way across the pan
   - ○ **D** by splashing it on each other

6. What does the word *squirmy* mean in this article?
   - ○ **A** twisting and turning
   - ○ **B** whimpering and crying
   - ○ **C** silent and scared
   - ○ **D** soft and quiet

Write a How-to Paragraph

Plan and Write The artwork in Lesson 10 shows children feeding a rabbit and a mother braiding her daughter's hair. Write a paragraph for your teacher telling how to care for someone or something. For example, you could explain how to help a child tie shoes. You could tell how to feed or brush a cat or give a dog a bath. Use the chart below to plan your paragraph. Then, write your paragraph on another sheet of paper.

Write your topic. List the materials you will need.

How-to Topic:	**Materials Needed:**

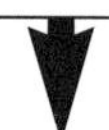

Write a topic sentence that tells what you will be explaining.

Topic Sentence:

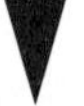

Tell about each step. Remember to use time-order words such as *first*, *next*, and *then*.

First Step:

Second Step:

Third Step:

Tell the last thing you do. Use time-order words such as *finally* or *last*.

Last Step:

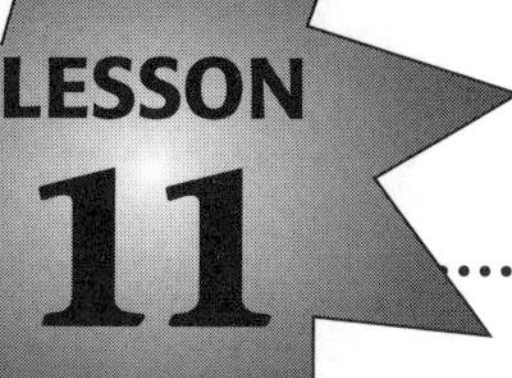

LESSON 11

People and Their Crops

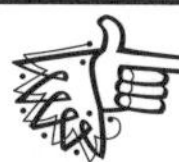

SET THE STAGE

Tell students that they will read an article entitled *People and Their Crops*. Then, use the Focus on Words section on this page to help them make predictions. You may wish to write the words on the chalkboard.

FOCUS ON WORDS

nomads   legumes

agriculture   leisure

crops

Make Predictions

RESOURCE:
TRANSPARENCIES
3-34, 3-35

Show the transparencies of the artworks by Giuseppe Arcimboldo, *Summer*, and *Dali Salad*, by Red Grooms (TRANSPARENCIES 3-34, 3-35). Ask: How does the subect of food show up in these two artworks? Have students think about the words as you read the title of the article again. Encourage them to predict how each word could be used in an article about the history of farming. Use the activity as a springboard to access what they already know about farming. (Possible student responses: Farming is concerned with the growing of <u>crops</u>. Another word for farming is <u>agriculture</u>.)

Read

Have students read the article on page 74. After they complete the first three paragraphs, pause. Discuss what they have learned so far. Ask them to predict how the world will change because of farming. Then, ask students to complete the article.

Respond

Help students complete the critical thinking questions on page 75. (See Answer Key, page 126.) Then lead them through the reading of the writing prompt on page 76. Discuss the subject they are to write about, the mode of writing, and the audience they are to address. Make sure they know how to use the graphic organizer to generate ideas for their written responses.

People and Their Crops

*S*ummer and *Dali Salad* makes us think about food. For thousands of years people have been thankful for the food they grow. Did you know that people did not always know how to raise crops for food?

For many thousands of years, people got food by hunting or fishing. They also gathered food from wild plants. However, this meant they had to live as nomads, moving from place to place, looking for food and water.

Then, about ten thousand years ago in the Middle East, people discovered they could grow plants for food! Soon fields of grains—wheat, oats, and legumes, such as peas and lentils—grew ripe in the sun. Grapes, olives, and figs were tended carefully. Farming meant a steady supply of food, and it gave people more free time. It was a better way of life than moving around all the time.

A new culture arose. People stopped moving and began living together in villages. They began to have leisure time. This free time allowed them to observe, think, and experiment. Over time, the results led to governments, arts, and sciences.

Throughout history, people have shown their gratitude for food by having feasts.

In the United States, many regions have their own special festivals in honor of a crop. Corn Fests, Apple Days, and Pumpkin Festivals are just a few of these special community celebrations. Our nation's biggest harvest festival is Thanksgiving Day. We prepare a feast and give thanks for all we have been given, especially agriculture and the blessings it offers.

Choose the best answer.

1. What does the word *nomads* mean?
   - ○ **A** plants that grow wild
   - ○ **B** farmers in the Middle East
   - ○ **C** people who wander in search of food
   - ○ **D** people who enjoy leisure time

2. Why did early people hunt and fish rather than farm?
   - ○ **A** They liked to eat meat and fish.
   - ○ **B** They did not know how to farm.
   - ○ **C** They didn't want to form villages and towns.
   - ○ **D** They felt it was easier to hunt and fish.

3. What change took place when people began to farm?
   - ○ **A** People had the leisure time to think.
   - ○ **B** People stopped eating meat or fish.
   - ○ **C** People gave up their spears and bows and arrows.
   - ○ **D** People could now travel from place to place.

4. Which kind of food did the first farmers grow?
   - ○ **A** fruit trees
   - ○ **B** leafy green plants
   - ○ **C** grains
   - ○ **D** root plants, like potatoes

5. According to the article, the most important crop festival today is
   - ○ **A** Thanksgiving Day.
   - ○ **B** The Pumpkin Festival.
   - ○ **C** The Crop Fest.
   - ○ **D** Apple Day.

6. What does the word *legume* mean in this article?
   - ○ **A** a tribe
   - ○ **B** a crop festival
   - ○ **C** a grain
   - ○ **D** a wild plant

Write a Thank-You Letter

Plan and Write Lesson 11 reminds us that we need to show gratitude for the good things we receive. Think of someone you want to thank. It could be a friend, a family member, or someone famous. Write a letter to this person thanking them for something they did or said that has made your life better or happier. Use the chart below to plan your letter. Then, write your letter on another sheet of paper.

Write the heading and greeting here.

Greeting: **Heading:**
                                                  Your address:

                                                  Today's date:

Dear ________________,
(Write the name of the person to whom you are writing.)

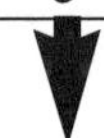

Tell the person why you are writing this letter. Explain why you are thankful.

First Paragraph:

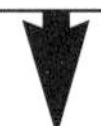

Describe your memory of what the person did for you or said to you that had an effect on your life. Give a specific example.

Second Paragraph:

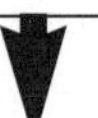

Tell the person why you wanted to express your gratitude for what he or she did for you.

Ending Paragraph:

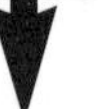

Write the closing in this space.

Closing:
Sincerely,

________________________________ (Write your signature here.)

The Awesome Pyramid

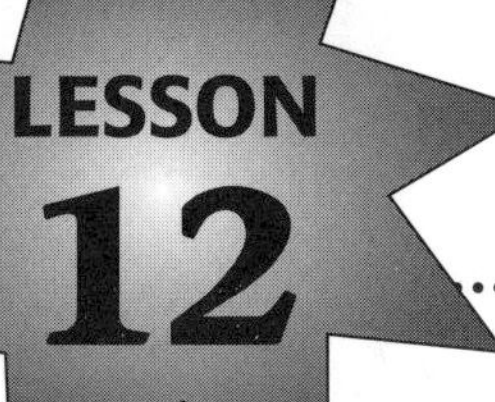

LESSON 12

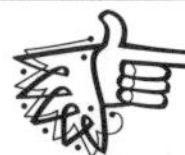

SET THE STAGE

Tell students that they will read an article entitled *The Awesome Pyramid*. Then, use the Focus on Words section on this page to help them make predictions. You may wish to write the words on the chalkboard.

FOCUS ON WORDS

monument   rectangle

architect   jeweled

Make Predictions

RESOURCE:
TRANSPARENCY
3-37

Show the transparency of *El Castillo/Pyramid of Kukulcan*. (TRANSPARENCY 3-37). Ask: How is this pyramid different from an Egyptian pyramid? What is its purpose? Have students think about the words as you read the title of the article. Encourage them to predict how each word could be used in an article about a pyramid. Use the activity as a springboard to access what they already know about pyramids. (Possible student response: A pyramid is a <u>monument</u>, a huge tombstone marking the grave of some important leader.)

Read

Have students read the article on page 78. After they complete the first two paragraphs, pause. Make sure students understand that the sides of the Great Pyramid have smooth lines. Ask students to predict what the rest of the article will be about. Then, ask students to complete the article.

Respond

Help students complete the critical thinking questions on page 79. (See Answer Key, page 126.) Then, lead them through the reading of the writing prompt on page 80. Discuss the subject they are to write about, the mode of writing, and the audience they are to address. Make sure they know how to use the graphic organizer to generate ideas for their written responses.

THE AWESOME PYRAMID

The El Castillo was built by Mayan Indians about a thousand years ago. This huge monument required years of labor by thousands of men. Why did ancient peoples, like the Mayans and the Egyptians, go to such trouble to build these stone wonders?

The Egyptians built pyramids to protect the tombs of their kings called pharaohs. The most famous pyramid in the world are the Great Pyramid of King Khufu in Egypt. There are two other pyramids built in the same area. King Khufu, his son, and his grandson were each buried in the very center of each of these three pyramids. Egyptian rulers were buried with many precious and beautiful items. Their bodies were laid in special coffins made of gold and decorated with jewels. Rulers feared that grave-robbers would break into their tombs and steal this wealth, so the passages to the tombs were later sealed off with huge rocks.

The pyramids found in South and Central America are different from those in Egypt. They are called step pyramids, and they angle upward, but not in a smooth line. Step pyramids developed from the burial practices of long ago. Early people used to place a solid rectangle of stone over a grave. This kept the sand covering the grave from blowing away. Later, they began to stack these rectangles on top of each other. Each rectangle was a little smaller than the one below it, forming steps up the sides. These were the first pyramids—the step pyramids.

El Castillo, the Mayan pyramid in Lesson 12, is a large step-pyramid built of earth and stone. The Mayan architects who created it dedicated it to their god, Kukulkan. El Castillo features a grand staircase in the center, leading to a temple at the top. A beautiful, jeweled throne sits inside. The temple is richly carved with pictures of gods. Pyramids were important to Mayans because they were centers of worship.

Name____ Date_____________ Class____________

Choose the best answer.

1. Why did the Egyptians seal up the passages in their pyramids?

○ **A** to keep grave robbers out

○ **B** to protect the soul of the pharaoh

○ **C** to keep people away from the tomb

○ **D** to keep sand and dust from the tomb

2. Why is El Castillo called a step pyramid?

○ **A** The sides of the pyramid go up in steps.

○ **B** The Mayans built a staircase on the front of it.

○ **C** Visitors must step in a pool before entering it.

○ **D** Each side of the pyramid is 20 steps wide.

3. If you climb the grand staircase of El Castillo, what will you find?

○ **A** a jeweled crown

○ **B** a temple

○ **C** a Mayan god

○ **D** a painting

4. The word *architect* in this passage means

○ **A** soldier.

○ **B** builder.

○ **C** priest.

○ **D** god.

5. What was the purpose of building the Mayan pyramids?

○ **A** They were tombs for Mayan pharaohs.

○ **B** They were museums for Mayan art.

○ **C** They were centers for Mayan worship.

○ **D** They were prisons for those captured in battle.

6. A rectangle has

○ **A** three sides.

○ **B** four sides.

○ **C** five sides.

○ **D** six sides.

Write a Comparison

Plan and Write The geodesic dome pictured in Lesson 12 (page 77 of the student textbook) is an unusual building. Think about what your school building looks like. Write two paragraphs for your teacher that compare and contrast your school and the geodesic dome. Use the Venn diagram below to plan your paragraphs. Then, write your paragraphs on another sheet of paper.

Geodesic Dome   **Both Buildings**   **Your School**

How dome is different from school

How both buildings are alike

How school is different from dome

Tips for Comparing

1. Begin the first paragraph with a topic sentence that tells what you are comparing. Give two or three details that tell how the two buildings are alike. Consider size, shape, materials, and purpose.

2. Begin the second paragraph with a topic sentence about differences. Consider the same features as above. Then, give two or three details about how the two buildings are different.

3. Use signal words such as *both* and *neither*.

4. End with a sentence that gives the main impression left by the buildings.

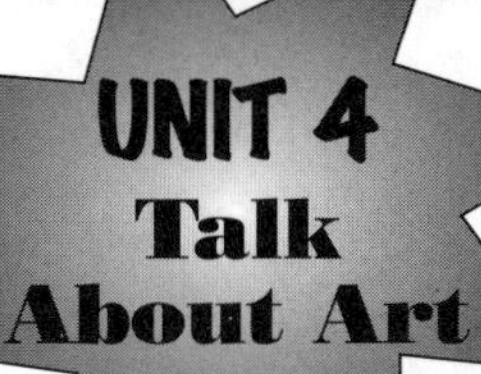

Games for Growing

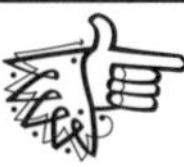

SET THE STAGE

Tell students that they will read an article entitled *Games for Growing*. Then, use the Focus on Words section on this page to help them make predictions. You may wish to write the words on the chalkboard.

FOCUS ON WORDS

survival   culture

warrior   accomplish

strategy

Make Predictions

RESOURCE:
TRANSPARENCY
3-41

Show the transparency of the painting *Pianist and Checker Players* by Henri Matiesse (TRANSPARENCY 3-41). Ask: When do you play games like this? (on rainy days) Discuss active games that can be played on sunny days. Have students think about the words as you read the title of the article. Encourage them to predict how each word could be used in an article about games. Use the activity as a springboard to access what they already know about games people play. (Possible student response: Games like chess can only be played well if you have a <u>strategy</u>.)

Read

Have students read the article on page 82. After they complete the first two paragraphs, pause. Make sure students understand that the Olympic games are still played today. Discuss the kind of skills these games still build. Then, have students complete the article.

Respond

Help students complete the critical thinking questions on page 83. (See Answer Key, page 126.) Then, lead them through the reading of the writing prompt on page 84. Discuss the subject they are to write about, the mode of writing, and the audience they are to address. Make sure they know how to use the graphic organizer to generate ideas for their written responses.

Games for Growing

In every culture, young and old enjoy playing games. In *The Chess Game* and *Pianist and Checker Players*, the artists show children playing games. Games give all of us a chance to spend time with friends or family and to have fun.

Have you every wondered why people play games? Why do children love them so? Long ago, games taught children the skills they needed for survival. Ancient cultures and tribes had many games of skill for young people. A game might teach the use of a bow and arrow in a culture of hunters. The first Olympic games were based on the skills that Greek warriors needed to defend their country.

Games of skill build your strength, but there is also joy in using the body. Have you ever noticed that you feel more energy after swimming or running or playing a game of volley-ball? People are made to be active, and physical activity feels good and helps keep you fit.

Many young people use physically active games to test themselves. It is pleasing to find out you are stronger or faster than you were last month. When you can finally beat your older brother or sister, you feel that you have accomplished something great.

We live in a time that requires us to think and figure out many problems. Certain kinds of games build mental strength. A game of dominos requires the use of math. The game of Scrabble uses spelling, language, and math skills. Chess and checkers require the use of strategy. The ability to think ahead and see the possible different results of different actions helps you solve problems in every area of life.

Games are a relaxing way to spend time with others. Games help us share laughter, too, and laughing is necessary for good mental health. So play hard and laugh a lot. It will make your life more enjoyable!

Choose the best answer. Fill in the circle next to your choice.

1. The word *survival* in this article means
   - ○ **A** staying alive.
   - ○ **B** winning the prize.
   - ○ **C** overcoming obstacles.
   - ○ **D** building skill.

2. How do people usually feel after playing a game?
   - ○ **A** They get very tired.
   - ○ **B** They have more energy.
   - ○ **C** They feel the same.
   - ○ **D** They feel sick.

3. In the fifth paragraph, the word *strategy* means
   - ○ **A** a game.
   - ○ **B** a plan.
   - ○ **C** a result.
   - ○ **D** a problem.

4. The first Olympic Games were based on the skills needed by
   - ○ **A** athletes.
   - ○ **B** women.
   - ○ **C** warriors.
   - ○ **D** slaves.

5. What is the fifth paragraph mainly about?
   - ○ **A** games that require physical strength
   - ○ **B** games that build survival skills
   - ○ **C** games that require mental strength
   - ○ **D** games that build up energy

6. Which of the following summarizes the last paragraph?
   - ○ **A** A place for everything, and everything in its place.
   - ○ **B** Look before you leap.
   - ○ **C** A penny saved is a penny earned.
   - ○ **D** Laughter is the best medicine.

Write a Fantasy Story

Plan and Write Picture a board game you enjoy. Now, imagine that the board and its parts have come to life. You have shrunk and become a part of this little world. Write a fantasy for your classmates that tells about what happens. What sort of characters have the playing pieces become? Use the story map below to plan your story. Then, write your story on another sheet of paper.

Name your characters, and tell how they came to life. Tell where and when this happened. Make sure your beginning sentence grabs your reader's attention.

Characters:	**Where:**
	When:

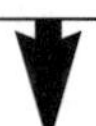

What problem do you have? Escaping from the game? Fitting in? Helping someone in trouble? Tell about it in a sentence.

Problem:

Tell what happens to you and the characters. Write the details in order.

First Event:

Second Event:

Third Event:

End the story by telling how the problem is solved.

Solution:

A Home Can Talk

 **SET THE STAGE**

Tell students that they will read an article entitled *A Home Can Talk*. Then, use the Focus on Words section on this page to help them make predictions. You may wish to write the words on the chalkboard.

FOCUS ON WORDS

personality   shrine

detail   sculpture

Make Predictions

RESOURCE:
TRANSPARENCY
3-50

Show the transparency of Beverly Buchanan's oil pastel *St. Simons* (TRANSPARENCY 3-50). Ask: Does this picture of two rural homes say anything about the people who live there? Have students think about the words as you read the title of the article. Encourage them to predict how each word could be used in an article about a home and what it says about those who live there. Use the activity as a springboard to access what they already know about the details of a home. (Possible student responses: The <u>personality</u> of the owner may show up in the color of a home.)

Read

Have students read the article on page 86. After they complete the first two paragraphs, pause. Ask students to explain what the author means by a home "talking." Ask them to restate what flowers in the yard "say," what clean windows "say," what toys in the yard "say." Then, have students complete the article.

Respond

Help students complete the critical thinking questions on page 87. ((See Answer Key, page 127.) Then, lead them through the reading of the writing prompt on page 88. Discuss the subject they are to write about, the mode of writing, and the audience they are to address. Make sure they know how to use the graphic organizer to generate ideas for their written responses.

A Home Can Talk

A home expresses a personality just as a person does. Walk through a neighborhood and pick a home. Look at the details. They say a lot about the people who live there.

First, if there is a yard, what is it like? A yard with lots of beautiful flowers and green grass says, "We love natural beauty. We are proud of our little piece of nature." Is the house clean and neat? A fresh coat of paint and clean windows show that the people inside want to present a shining "face" to the world. Toys in the yard say, "This home is lived in. We want our children to have happy memories of home."

Some homes express personality in small ways. A brightly colored flag flies in the wind. Wind chimes tinkle whenever the wind blows. These little touches show that these people want nature to help them make art. Bird feeders show a family reaching out to touch nature. They are grateful for wild things.

Some people put statues in the yard. A silly carved goose with wooden wings that turn in the breeze shows a sense of humor. A statue of a saint is like a little shrine that connects the owner with a faith. A piece of sculpture shows appreciation for what an artist can make.

Then there is the front door. A bright red front door asks to be noticed. A door with a pretty window looks out in welcome. Is the front door decorated? Many people hang a holiday wreath on the door. Sometimes the windows are covered with pictures made by children or grandchildren. Such details can tell you about people you have never met.

Name______________________________________ Date_____________ Class_____________

Choose the best answer. Fill in the circle next to your choice.

1. What is the main idea of this article?
   ○ **A** The things you place in your front yard show your personality.
   ○ **B** A bird feeder shows that you love nature.
   ○ **C** A home expresses a family's thoughts and feelings.
   ○ **D** A front door shows whether you like people.

2. The word *shrine* in this article means
   ○ **A** a wind chime.
   ○ **B** a bird feeder.
   ○ **C** a religious statue.
   ○ **D** a silly statue.

3. Suppose you saw a house with a fenced-in yard and young puppies at play. What would such things "say" about the people who live here?
   ○ **A** They like their privacy.
   ○ **B** They enjoy animals.
   ○ **C** They believe in "No Trespassing."
   ○ **D** They are wealthy.

4. Which of the following is an example of a sculpture?
   ○ **A** a flag on the roof
   ○ **B** a wreath on the door
   ○ **C** pictures in the windows
   ○ **D** a statue in the yard

5. According to the article, people often celebrate holidays by
   ○ **A** displaying a wreath.
   ○ **B** planting a tree.
   ○ **C** painting the house.
   ○ **D** hanging a wind chime.

6. The word *detail* means
   ○ **A** price.
   ○ **B** rules.
   ○ **C** a small part.
   ○ **D** facts.

Write a Realistic Story

Plan and Write Beverly Buchanan likes the homes she draws to tell a story. Think about a home where you would like to live. (Draw a picture of it if you wish.) Write a story for your teacher that tells about a day in that home. Let the house talk about itself and the people who live in it. Use the story map below to plan your paragraphs. Then, write your story on another sheet of paper.

Name your characters: <u>you</u>, <u>the house</u>, and <u>those who live with you</u>. Write a sentence to describe each character.

Is the home in the city, on a mountain, or by the sea? Is it summer, winter, spring, or fall?

Characters:

You:

The house:

Those who live with you:

Setting:

Where and When:

What problem must be solved? Is there a fire or a storm, or do the people have a problem? Tell about it in a sentence.

Problem:

What happens to the characters on this day? What do they do? (Include details that show the personality of the home, as well as the people who live there).

First Event:

Second Event:

Third Event:

How does the story end? Tell how the problem is solved.

Solution:

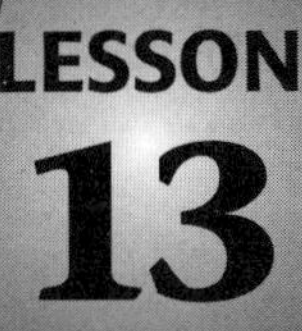

LESSON 13

What Quilts Express

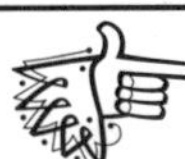

SET THE STAGE

Tell students that they will read an article titled *What Quilts Express*. Then, use the Focus on Words section on this page to help them make predictions. You may wish to write the words on the chalkboard.

FOCUS ON WORDS

quilts   geometric

visual rhythm   society

traditional

Make Predictions

RESOURCE:
TRANSPARENCY
3-42

Show the transparency of Faith Ringgold's quilt *Harlem Renaissance Party: Bitter Nest, Part II*. (TRANSPARENCY 3-42). Ask: What kind of story does this quilt tell? Have students think about the words as you read the title of the article. Encourage them to predict how each word could be used in an article about quilts and what they express. Use the activity as a springboard to access what they already know about quilts. (Possible student responses: A <u>quilt</u> can be made up of <u>geometric</u> shapes of fabrics arranged in patterns.)

Read

Have students read the article on page 90. After they complete the first two paragraphs, pause. Ask students to refer to the quilt on page 90 and explain where the pictures and the words are. Next, ask students to predict what the rest of the article will be about. Then, have them complete the article.

Respond

Help students complete the critical thinking questions on page 91. (See Answer Key, page 127.) Then, lead them through the reading of the writing prompt on page 92. Discuss the subject they are to write about, the mode of writing, and the audience they are to address. Make sure they know how to use the graphic organizer to generate ideas for their written responses.

What Quilts Express

Are there any quilts in your home? If there are, they may have stories to tell. A quilt is both an artwork and a blanket. It can also be a little piece of history.

Faith Ringgold's quilt tells a story in pictures and words. Her quilt shows great African American writers and artists around a dinner table. Colorful geometric patterns make a frame around the people and show that they belong together.

Most quilts use a pattern of blocks that repeat the same design. The repeated lines and colors, give a quilt a strong visual rhythm. The design may be a geometric shape or something well loved from nature.

Pioneer women made thousands of "Log Cabin" quilts. A design called "Abe Lincoln's Platform" was a way of saying that you were for Union during the Civil War. Women were not allowed to vote then, but they showed their thoughts about society in the quilts they made.

Quilts may also mark important events in a family. A birth of a baby or a wedding called for the gift of a quilt. A group of friends and relatives might make an "Album" quilt. It told a part of a person's or a family's personal history. A mother might make a "Freedom" quilt for her son when he reached a certain age and started a life of his own. Quilts like these have great meaning for families.

Today's quiltmakers use traditional patterns to honor the past. They also create new effects using skills from painting and printmaking as well as computer design. However, old quilts are appreciated for the history and art they combine. They were made by women of long ago with love and care. They tell those of us who live today how our ancestors lived.

Name_________________________________ Date___________ Class____________

Choose the best answer. Fill in the circle next to your choice.

1. A quilt is a

○ **A** blanket.

○ **B** painting.

○ **C** skirt.

○ **D** portrait.

2. A geometric pattern is a pattern based on

○ **A** primary and secondary colors.

○ **B** birds, bees, and flowers.

○ **C** faces of people from the past.

○ **D** squares and triangles and other shapes.

3. Why did the women of long ago spend so much time making quilts?

○ **A** A quilt was necessary to keep warm.

○ **B** A quilt could be sold for a great deal of money.

○ **C** A quilt could tell what a woman believed in.

○ **D** A quilt could be washed and dried easily.

4. How do modern quiltmakers create different effects?

○ **A** They use traditional patterns.

○ **B** They may use computer-made designs.

○ **C** They make quilts by hand.

○ **D** They make quilts that tell a story.

5. The word *society* in this article means

○ **A** people of the community.

○ **B** a friend.

○ **C** very rich people.

○ **D** world population.

6. We treasure the quilts made long ago because of their

○ **A** free spirit.

○ **B** fine workmanship.

○ **C** history.

○ **D** humor.

Write About a Quilt Design

Plan and Write Imagine you are going to make a quilt to represent your family. What design would you create? It should have lines, shapes, and colors that suit the interests and personality of your family. (Draw your design on scratch paper.) Write a paragraph for a friend describing your design and explaining why it suits your family. Use the chart below to plan your paragraph. Then, write your paragraph on another sheet of paper.

First, write a topic sentence that tells in what way the design suits your family.

Topic Sentence:

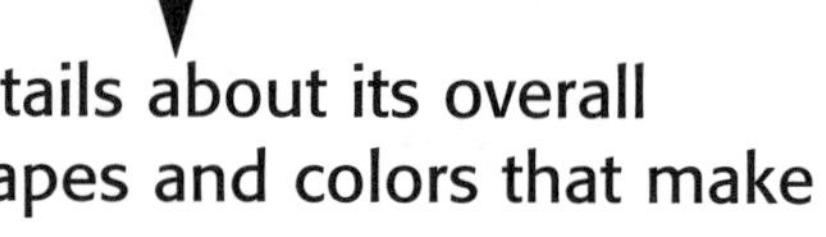

Next, describe the design. Give details about its overall impression. Describe the lines, shapes and colors that make up the design of the quilt.

Overall Impression:

Lines, Shapes, Colors:

Mention specific details and tell how they represent your family. For example, a green stalk could show a family history of farming. Explain what the design means to you.

Details:

What They Mean:

Write an ending sentence. Tell where your family would keep this quilt and why.

Ending Sentence:

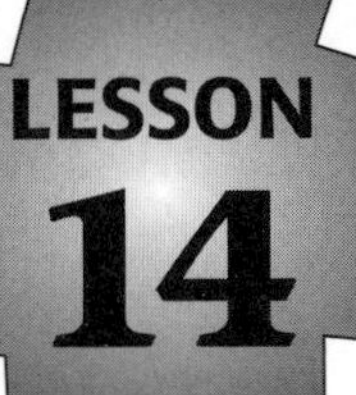

LESSON 14

Photographs of People

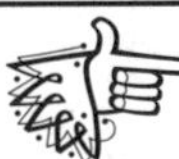

SET THE STAGE

Tell students that they will read an article entitled *Photographs of People*. Then, use the Focus on Words on this page to help them make predictions. You may wish to write the words on the chalkboard.

FOCUS ON WORDS

photographs   candid

portrait   composed

Make Predictions

RESOURCE:
TRANSPARENCY
3-47

Show the transparency of the photograph of Shawn Nixon in *Boxcar Pose* (TRANSPARENCY 3-47). Ask: Why do people find the picture of this young girl both odd and pleasing? Have students think about the words as you read the title of the article. Encourage them to predict how each word could be used in an article about photographs of people. Use the activity as a springboard to access what they already know about photographs. (Possible student response: A <u>candid</u> photograph usually looks more natural because the person doesn't know a camera is around.)

Read

Have students read the article on page 94. After they complete the first three paragraphs, pause. Ask students to think about any "portraits" taken of them, such as class pictures. Ask whether or not they "looked their best," as the article suggests. Lead students to see that photography, as discussed in this lesson, is not concerned with "glamour shots" but with revealing or presenting a person's true self. Then, have them complete the article.

Respond

Help students complete the critical thinking questions on page 95. (See Answer Key, page 127.) Then, lead them through the reading of the writing prompt on page 96. Discuss the subject they are to write about, the mode of writing, and the audience they are to address. Make sure they know how to use the graphic organizer to generate ideas for their written responses.

Integrated Reading and Writing: Grade 3

Photographs of People

Do you have photo albums at home? They tell many stories. Perhaps one tells the story of a fun vacation. Another might tell the story of how you have grown and changed since you were born.

Because they stop time, photographs help us notice details. In our everyday rush, we sometimes don't see other persons clearly. Study a picture of someone you know well and see if you notice new things. Maybe there is kindness in the eyes that you never noticed before. Maybe you never realized how many freckles your sister has.

A camera can also show personality. A good portrait is composed in a way that makes a person look his or her best. It lets us see what the person is really like. A fun-loving, outgoing nature shines through in a hearty laugh. A quiet, dreamy nature becomes clear through soft light, shadows, and a slight smile. Bright colors and lots of jewelry might show someone who is the life of the party.

A portrait may include objects that show something about the subject. A grandma who loves baseball might be photographed in her favorite baseball cap. A dad who loves cooking might be snapped in the kitchen making a pizza.

Candid shots can be the best of all. These are pictures taken in a moment of action. The subject does not know the picture is being taken. A shot of a soccer goalie leaping for a ball can show energy, skill, and effort. A shot of a toddler can show freshness and wonder.

A photograph has a sort of magic that lasts. In fifty years, that picture of the goalie may make a child see his grandfather in a whole new light.

Choose the best answer. Fill in the circle next to your choice.

1. The word *portrait* in this article means

○ **A** A a posed photograph of a person.

○ **B** an oil painting of a person.

○ **C** a candid photo of a person in action.

○ **D** a large color photo of a home.

2. The main idea of this article can be stated as follows:

○ **A** Photo albums are an excellent way to record family fun.

○ **B** A good photograph can show someone's inner personality.

○ **C** Photographs are valuable a long time after they are taken.

○ **D** A good photograph shows lots of detail.

3. A candid photograph is one that is taken

○ **A** in black and white.

○ **B** without the subject knowing it.

○ **C** and enlarged at least two times.

○ **D** outdoors.

4. The word *composed* in this article means

○ **A** planned.

○ **B** studied.

○ **C** filmed.

○ **D** saved.

5. Why do portraits often include objects owned by the person?

○ **A** Certain objects can show what a person likes to do.

○ **B** Objects can provide balance to the picture.

○ **C** Objects can make the person look better.

○ **D** Portraits do not include objects.

6. Which of the following summarizes the last paragraph?

○ **A** Your children will be glad you saved your old photographs.

○ **B** Anyone in sports should save action photographs.

○ **C** Photographs can have a certain magic.

○ **D** Photographs will last at least fifty years.

Writing a Letter to Persuade

Plan and Write Who would you like to photograph? Write a letter persuading the person to let you make a photographic portrait. Decide on the place, clothes, and objects that you want to include. Convince the person that your choices best match his or her personality. Use the chart below to plan your letter. Then, write your letter on another sheet of paper.

Write the heading and greeting here.

Greeting:	Heading:
	Today's Date:
	Your address:
Dear _________________,	
(Write the name of the person to whom you are writing.)	

▼

Begin by telling the person what you want to do and why. Explain why the portrait is important and why you are the person to do it.

First Paragraph:

▼

Describe the setting for the picture and the objects you want to include. Explain why these suit the subject's personality or interests.

Second Paragraph:

Setting/Reasons: Objects/Reasons:

▼

Describe how you will pose your subject. Describe what he or she will wear. Give reasons why these are good choices.

Third Paragraph:

Pose/Reasons: Clothes/Reasons:

▼

Tell your subject why he or she should choose you to make the portrait.

Ending Sentence:

▼

Write the closing in this space.

Closing:

Your friend,

_________________   (Write your signature here.)

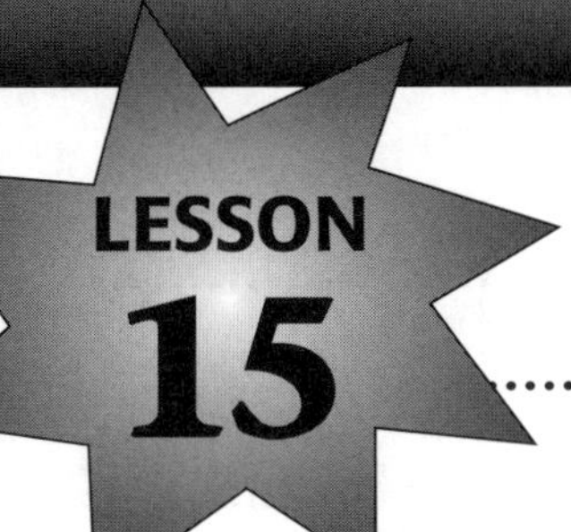

LESSON 15

The Computer and Industrial Design

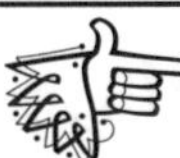

SET THE STAGE

Tell students that they will read an article entitled *The Computer and Industrial Design*. Then, use the Focus on Words section on this page to help them make predictions. You may wish to write the words on the chalkboard.

FOCUS ON WORDS

manufactured

CAD–Computer Aided Design

models   **accuracy**

Make Predictions

RESOURCE:
TRANSPARENCY
3-55

Show the transparency of two different styles of telephones (TRANSPARENCY 3-55). Ask: How has the design of the telephone changed over the years? Have students think about the words as you read the title of the article. Encourage them to predict how each word could be used in an article about the computer and how it helps design things we use, like the telephone. Use the activity as a springboard to access what they already know about computers. (Possible student response: The computer may be able to help a designer make a <u>model</u> of a product.)

Read

Have students read the article on page 98. After they complete the first two paragraphs, pause. Make sure students understand what an industrial designer does. (Such a person thinks about how a product looks, as well as how it feels in your hand and does its job for you.) Ask students to predict what else they might learn about industrial design in the rest of the article. Then, have them complete the article.

Respond

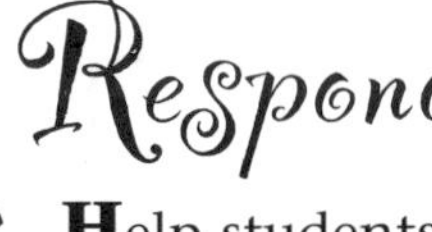

Help students complete the critical thinking questions on page 99. (See Answer Key, page 127.) Then, lead them through the reading of the writing prompt on page 100. Discuss the subject they are to write about, the mode of writing, and the audience they are to address. Make sure they know how to use the graphic organizer to generate ideas for their written responses.

The Computer and Industrial Design

The objects that you use every day were designed by experts. Think of some objects you use often—a toothbrush, a tennis racket, a backpack, a plastic water bottle. Industrial designers make these objects the best they can be.

It takes a lot of careful planning before a product can be manufactured. The designer must answer questions such as these: Are the size and shape right?

Will the material—metal, plastic, wood—work for this object? Is the object easy to use? Will people like the way it looks? Can it be made easily and cheaply?

The computer has changed industrial design. Computer-aided design (CAD) lets designers create more complex objects and learn more about them.

With CAD, designers create models on the computer. They enter geometric information using the computer keyboard. This information tells the computer to create points, lines, circles, curves, and rounded corners. Designers use these pieces to build boxes, cylinders, spheres, and cones on the screen. The model appears in the form of shaded images. The computer can be directed to make copies of the shapes, rotate them, and change their size.

Earlier in this century, designers had to make drawings by hand. That took a lot of time. Furthermore, the drawings could not answer all questions about the design because they were flat. Today, CAD creates models that can be studied inside and out. CAD helps the designer-operator create and make changes with great speed and accuracy.

The computer can also show weight, volume, surface area, and other information about the product. A shoe designer can see what happens inside the sole of a shoe as it moves with a foot. A doctor can see how a new tool works in an operation. All this computer work saves time, money, effort—and even lives.

Integrated Reading and Writing: Grade 3

Name____ Date_____________ Class____________

Choose the best answer. Fill in the circle next to your choice.

1. Which statement gives the main idea of this article?

○ **A** Today, industrial designers set up their models on computers.

○ **B** The computer helps industrial designers learn more and work faster.

○ **C** Even your toothbrush gets attention from an industrial designer.

○ **D** A designer can create boxes, cylinders, spheres, and cones on a computer.

2. The word *manufactured* in this article means

○ **A** designed.

○ **B** produced.

○ **C** packaged.

○ **D** checked.

3. Why does a shoe designer study a product "inside and out"?

○ **A** to find out what will happen when someone walks in the shoe

○ **B** to learn how many sizes of the shoe can be made

○ **C** to find out how many companies can manufacture the shoe

○ **D** to learn what colors can be used on the inside of the shoe

4. In this article, the word *accuracy* means

○ **A** flat.

○ **B** exact.

○ **C** fast.

○ **D** complex.

5. In the early 1900's, how did designers create their designs?

○ **A** They used computers.

○ **B** They created solid models.

○ **C** They made drawings by hand.

○ **D** They explained their designs.

6. According to the article, which one would NOT be part of a toy designer's plan?

○ **A** the size and shape of a new toy

○ **B** how the new toy looks

○ **C** which stores will sell the new toy

○ **D** what materials will be used to make the new toy

Write About Computer Words

Plan and Write Computers have changed the way the world works. They have also changed our language. They have introduced new words into English and they have given familiar words new meanings. Write a paper for your teacher about some of the words we use in the computer age. You may choose from the words in the word bank or other words you know. Use the chart below to plan your paragraphs. Then, write your paragraphs on another sheet of paper.

Word Box	
mouse	virus
memory	keyboard
import/export	file
drag and drop	icon
floppy disk	hard drive
scanner	modem

Write a paragraph explaining that the computer has changed the meaning of some familiar words. (Example: a mouse) Choose a few words from the word bank. Write a sentence about each one, explaining how the computer has changed its meaning.

First Paragraph:

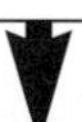

Explain some new words that people have had to learn because of computers. Use more words from the word bank as examples.

Second Paragraph:

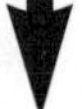

Finally, write a short paragraph that looks to the future of computer words.

Third Paragraph:

UNIT 5
Talk About Art

The Science and Art of Neon

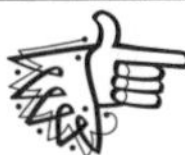

SET THE STAGE

Tell students that they will read an article entitled *The Science and Art of Neon*. Then, use the Focus on Words section on this page to help them make predictions. You may wish to write the words on the chalkboard.

FOCUS ON WORDS

neon   distill

electrons   stable

Make Predictions

RESOURCE:
TRANSPARENCY
3-51

Show the transparency of Ben Livingston's *Neon Mural* (TRANSPARENCY 3-51). Ask: What is a neon sign? Where have you seen one and what did it look like? Have students think about the words as you read the title of the article. Encourage them to predict how each word could be used in an article about a how artists create art with neon. Use the activity as a springboard to access what they already know about neon signs. (Possible student response: Perhaps neon is combined with <u>electrons</u> to make brightly colored signs.

Read

Have students read the article on page 102. After they complete the first three paragraphs, pause. Ask students to explain how neon is prepared and how it is made to glow. Ask students to predict what the rest of the article will be about. Then, have them complete the article.

Respond

Help students complete the critical thinking questions on page 103. (See Answer Key, page 127.) Then, lead them through the reading of the writing prompt on page 104. Discuss the subject they are to write about, the mode of writing, and the audience they are to address. Make sure they know how to use the graphic organizer to generate ideas for their written responses.

The Science and Art of Neon

Have you have ever seen a city lit up with neon signs? If you have, you know about this night magic. Signs of bright orange, purple, green, pink, and yellow glow like space candy. Glass tubes in many shapes and colors blink and flash. Since their invention in the 1920s, neon signs have changed the look of cities and towns the world over.

How are neon signs made? First, the neon must be prepared. Neon is a gas found in the earth's air. In 88,000 pounds of air, there is 1 pound of neon. It is lighter than air and it has no odor. Neon is obtained by distilling liquid air. When you distill something, you make it more pure and concentrated.

After the neon is obtained, it is placed in a special tube with electricity flowing through it. Electricity is actually a current of electrons, or tiny bits of atoms, which have a charge. As these tiny bits of energy hit the tiny bits of gas, they make the neon glow.

If you were able to touch the glass tube, you would find it cool. Neon produces cool light because its atoms are very stable. They do not want to change. Neon light is a bright orange red. However, other neon light colors are made by adding tiny amounts of other gases to the tube.

Many neon light makers of the past were artists in their own ways. They made light-filled figures, words, and shapes that would draw the eye. Most people who bought neon signs wanted to use them to advertise. Neon signs appeared in the windows of stores, restaurants, and theaters.

Neon signs express something bright and bold that suits the character of optimistic people in the computer age. Today, few people make neon signs, but we appreciate the art that goes into making them.

Choose the best answer. Fill in the circle next to your choice.

1. The word *distill* in this article means

○ **A** charge with electricity.

○ **B** insert color.

○ **C** make pure.

○ **D** expand.

2. The word *stable* in this article means

○ **A** a shelter for horses.

○ **B** not easily changed.

○ **C** sensible.

○ **D** easily excited.

3. The main reason for making neon signs is

○ **A** to express art.

○ **B** to decorate.

○ **C** to advertise.

○ **D** to light up the night.

4. What effect does electricity have on neon gas?

○ **A** It gives neon color.

○ **B** It makes the neon sparkle.

○ **C** It charges the neon.

○ **D** It brightens the neon.

5. When were neon signs invented?

○ **A** early in this century.

○ **B** late in this century.

○ **C** midway through this century.

○ **D** in the previous century.

6. How do scientist make neon change colors?

○ **A** They add other gases to it.

○ **B** They distill it.

○ **C** They inject additional electricity into it.

○ **D** They insert vegetable dyes into the neon.

Compare and Contrast Homes

Plan and Write The oil pastel, *St. Simons*, shows two poor rural homes. Compare them to your home or to other homes. Write a paper for your teacher telling how these homes are alike and how they are different. Use the Venn diagram and tips below to help you plan your paragraphs. Then, write your paragraphs on another sheet of paper.

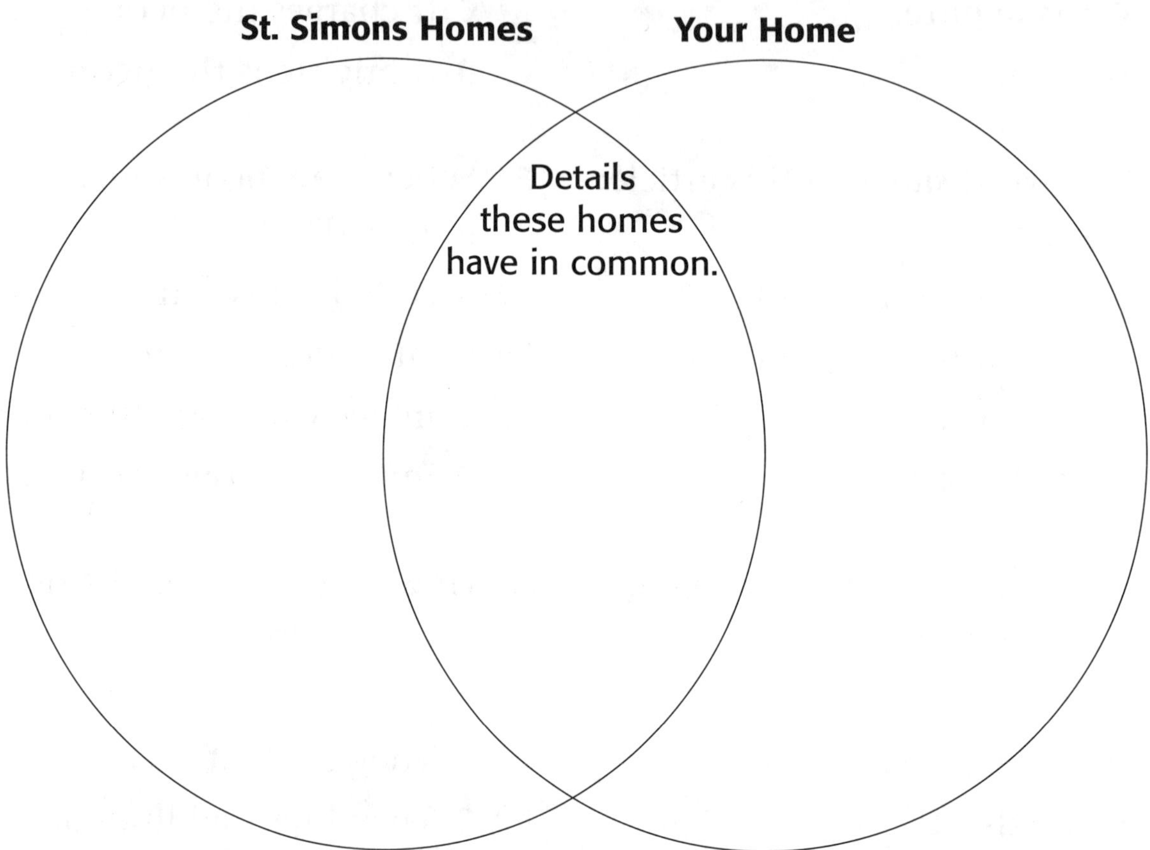

HINT: Details to consider: shape/form; colors; building materials; entrance/ windows; what happens inside; how people feel about the home(s).

TIPS FOR COMPARING AND CONTRASTING

1. Begin the first paragraph with a topic sentence telling what you are comparing and contrasting. Give two or three details that tell how your home is different from the homes in St. Simons.

2. Begin your second paragraph with a topic sentence, too. Then, give two or three details that tell how the homes are alike.

3. Use signal words such as *both* and *neither*.

4. Write a conclusion telling which home you like best and why.

A New Land, a New Home

👉 SET THE STAGE

Tell students that they will read an article entitled *A New Land, a New Home*. Then, use the Focus on Words section on this page to help them make predictions. You may wish to write the words on the chalkboard.

FOCUS ON WORDS

native land   emigrant

opportunity   adjustment

Make Predictions

RESOURCE:
TRANSPARENCY
3-50

Show the transparency of Yang Fang Nhu's *Story Cloth* (TRANSPAREN-CY 3-50). Ask: What story can you figure out as you look at this cloth? Have students think about the words as you read the title of the article. Encourage them to predict how each word could be used in an article about people who move to a new land to make a new home there. Use the activity as a springboard to access what they already know about emigrants. (Possible student response: An <u>emigrant</u> is someone who moves from his or her own country to another land.)

Read

Have students read the article on page 104. After they complete the first two paragraphs, pause. Ask students to think of any newcomers they may know. Perhaps a relative, friend, or neighbor is from another country. Discuss the kinds of problems this person has faced adjusting to the United States. Then, ask students to complete the article.

Respond

Help students complete the critical thinking questions on page 105. (See Answer key, page 127.) Then, lead them through the reading of the writing prompt on page 106. Discuss the subject they are to write about, the mode of writing, and the audience they are to address. Make sure they know how to use the graphic organizer to generate ideas for their written responses.

A New Land, a New Home

Yang Fang Nhu's story cloth tells how the Hmong moved from their home in China to Southeast Asia. Nhu herself is a Hmong woman who moved from Laos to the United States. Her rhythmic style of weaving is part of the tradition of the Hmong, handed down to her by her mother. Nhu used this skill to tell the story of her people in a beautiful way.

A person who leaves his or her native land for a another country is an *emigrant*. Most people prefer to live in their native land, the land where they were born. However, some people are driven from their homeland by war or hunger. In the early 1800's, the potato crop failed in Ireland and many Irish had to leave to keep from starving. Some people emigrate because they want the opportunity for a better life. Many people come to the United States for freedom and a chance to own land.

When they arrive in a new land, newcomers must adjust to many strange ways. If they are lucky, the landscape, language, and customs are much like those of the old country. Sometimes, however, the adjustment is difficult. A new language may have to be learned. Strange foods and clothing styles can be a shock. Emigrants may have to learn a new way to make a living. For example, a man who has always farmed rice may have to learn to work in a factory.

Sometimes new people are not accepted by some people in the new country because of their differences. Emigrants bring the customs of their homeland with them. Over time, they adopt many of the ways of the new country. However, they also keep some of the old ways. A special dance, a recipe for an ethnic dish, or a song from the old country brings comfort and enriches the new home.

Choose the best answer. Fill in the circle next to your choice.

1. According to the article, why did Yang Fang Nhu create a story cloth?
   ○ **A** to remember the past
   ○ **B** to help newcomers to this country
   ○ **C** to earn money
   ○ **D** to enter an art contest

2. An *opportunity* according to this article means
   ○ **A** an opinion.
   ○ **B** a burden.
   ○ **C** a chance.
   ○ **D** a job.

3. According to the author, the adjustment to a new country will be especially difficult
   ○ **A** if the government in the new country is different.
   ○ **B** if the language in the new country is different.
   ○ **C** if the art work in the new country is different.
   ○ **D** if the sports played in the new country are different.

4. An *emigrant* is a person who
   ○ **A** leaves his or her native land.
   ○ **B** looks for new opportunities.
   ○ **C** is willing to try a new job.
   ○ **D** enjoys a challenge.

5. According to the article, what can bring comfort to people who move to a new country?
   ○ **A** new opportunities for work
   ○ **B** songs, dances, or food from the old country
   ○ **C** customs in the new country
   ○ **D** a chance to earn more money than in the old country

6. What is your *native land*?
   ○ **A** the land you live in
   ○ **B** the land your family comes from
   ○ **C** the land where you hold citizenship
   ○ **D** the land where you were born

Write about Likes and Dislikes

Plan and Write The trip to a new home must have been an adventure for the Hmong. Think of a time when you had a big change. Maybe you had to move to a new home, go to a new school, or deal with a new situation. Write a paragraph to a friend telling what you liked and disliked about your experience. Use the chart to help you plan your paragraph. Then, write your paragraph on a another sheet of paper.

Tell about the event that changed your life. Write an interesting opening sentence that gives the general idea of how you felt.

Opening Sentence:

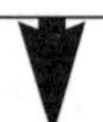

Write about the most important thing you liked about this change. Then, write about another thing you liked. Give a reason for each.

Most important thing I liked and why:

Another thing I liked and why:

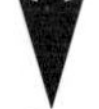

Write the most important thing you did not like about the change. Then, write about another thing you did not like. Give a reason for each.

Most important thing I did not like and why:

Another thing I did not like and why:

End your paragraph. Restate your main idea.

Ending Sentence:

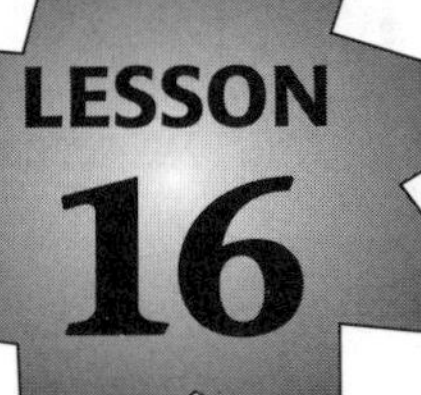

LESSON 16

A Journal from Java

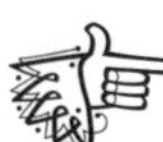 **SET THE STAGE**

Tell students that they will read an article entitled *A Journal from Java*. Then, use the Focus on Words section on this page to help them make predictions. You may wish to write the words on the chalkboard.

FOCUS ON WORDS

batik	sizing
glazes	dye
tjanting	

Make Predictions

RESOURCE:
TRANSPARENCY
3-50

Show the transparency of Yang Fang Nhu's *Hmong Skirt* (TRANSPARENCY 3-50). Ask: Which colors do you see on this skirt? Which design do you like best? Have students think about the words as you read the title of the article. Encourage them to predict how each word could be used in journal entries by a young girl telling how she made a batik skirt. Use the activity as a springboard to access what they already know about the art of making batik. (Possible student response: The young girl would need to use <u>dye</u> on the skirt.)

Read

Have students read the article on page 110. After they complete the first two paragraphs, pause. Discuss what they have learned so far about the art of making batik. What will they probably read about in the rest of the article? Ask students to make predictions. Then, ask students to complete the article.

Respond

Help students complete the critical thinking questions on page 111. (See Answer Key, page 127.) Then, lead them through the reading of the writing prompt on page 112. Discuss the subject they are to write about, the mode of writing, and the audience they are to address. Make sure they know how to use the graphic organizer to generate ideas for their written responses.

A Journal from Java

March 5: Today, Mama let me work with her making batik! First, we had to prepare the cloth. It was white and stiff. Our job was to soften the cotton fibers. To do this, we washed the cloth in a tub and let it dry. We did this three times. In the last washing, we added sticky starch. Mama said this is sizing. It glazes and fills the small openings in the fabric.

March 6: It takes so much to get ready! Today, we beat the cloth with sticks. This sounds funny, but we had to do this to make the cloth smooth and soft. Now it is ready for the dye. The next step is not coloring, though. It is drawing! We drew a beautiful design of fish and plants underwater. I can't wait for tomorrow!

March 7: At last we were able to color the cotton. First, we put hot melted wax on the design. To do this, Mama used the tjanting tool. You have to be careful not to let the copper bowl filled with wax burn you! Spouts of different sizes let you control how much wax goes onto the cloth and where. Mama let me use some of her brushes and pens to put wax on some patterns. Finally, she smiled at me and nodded. The deep blue dye was ready in a big pot, and in went the cloth! After awhile, we took it out to dry.

March 8: Today, we scraped the wax off the dry cloth. The design of the underwater fish and plants was still white. That's because the wax resisted the dye. The background, however, was blue, as blue as the ocean! That's because we kept that part of the cloth unwaxed.

But who wants white plants in a beautiful blue ocean? We got our hot wax ready again. This time we covered the fish and kept the plants unwaxed. We dipped the cloth in green dye to color the plants. We will keep on doing this until every fish, rock, and plant is colored just the way we want it.

Name____ Date______________ Class______________

Choose the best answer. Fill in the circle next to your choice.

1. Who is the speaker in this story?
- ○ **A** the president of Java
- ○ **B** a collector of art works
- ○ **C** a child about your age
- ○ **D** a woman who makes batik

2. What will the cloth look like when it is finished?
- ○ **A** a green cloth with red fish, blue plants, and green water
- ○ **B** a blue cloth with green plants and fish and rocks in other colors
- ○ **C** a white cloth with red fish, green plants, and blue water
- ○ **D** a blue cloth with red fish, blue plants, and green water

3. When did the women draw their design on the cloth?
- ○ **A** after they washed the cloth
- ○ **B** after they beat the cloth with sticks
- ○ **C** before they washed the cloth
- ○ **D** after they used the tjanting tool

4. According to the article, sizing is a
- ○ **A** cotton fabric.
- ○ **B** a deep blue dye.
- ○ **C** hot wax.
- ○ **D** sticky starch.

5. When was the fabric put into the big pot of blue dye?
- ○ **A** before the design was drawn
- ○ **B** after the wax was put on it
- ○ **C** before the fabric was washed
- ○ **D** after the cloth was beaten with sticks

6. What does the word *dye* mean in this article?
- ○ **A** something used to color cloth
- ○ **B** something used to soften cloth
- ○ **C** something used to wax cloth
- ○ **D** something used to design cloth

Write a How-to Paragraph

Plan and Write Weaving or dying cloth takes many careful steps. What do you know how to make or do? Write a paragraph for your classmates explaining how to make something from fabric, paper, cardboard, or wood. Include all the steps and tell about each step in order. Use the chart below to plan your paragraph. Then, write your paragraph on a another sheet of paper.

Write your topic. List all the materials you will need.

How-to Topic:	**Materials Needed:**

Write a topic sentence that tells what you will be explaining.

Topic Sentence:

Tell about each step. Use time-order words such as *first*, *next*, and *then*.

First Step:

Second Step:

Third Step:

Tell the last thing you do. Use time-order words such as *finally* or *last*.

Last step:

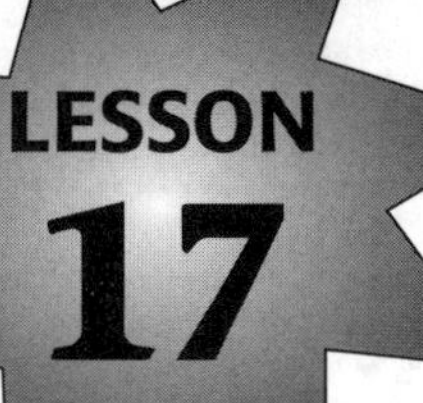

Phones Yesterday, Today, and Tomorrow

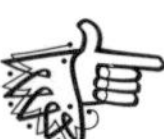

SET THE STAGE

Tell students that they will read an article titled *Telephones: Yesterday, Today, and Tomorrow*. Then, use the Focus on Words section on this page to help them make predictions. You may wish to write the words on the chalkboard.

FOCUS ON WORDS

call box	transmitter
earpiece	sleek
cordless	headset
videophone	

Make Predictions

RESOURCE:
TRANSPARENCY
3-55

Show the transparency of *Trimline telephone, "500" Type Desk Set telephone* (TRANSPARENCY 3-55). Ask: Has telephone design changed since these phones were designed? Have students think about the words as you read the title of the article. Encourage them to predict how each word could be used in an article about the history of telephone design. Use the activity as a springboard to access what they already know about telephones. (Possible student response: The trimline phone has a <u>sleek</u> design compared to the desk set phone.)

Read

Have students read the article on page 114. After they complete the first two paragraphs, pause. Discuss the first telephone with students. Ask them to predict how the rest of the article will proceed. Then, have them complete the article.

Respond

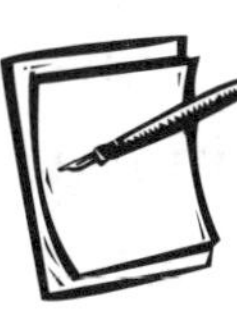

Help students complete the critical thinking questions on page 115. (See Answer Key page 127.) Then, lead them through the reading of the writing prompt on page 116. Discuss the subject they are to write about, the mode of writing, and the audience they are to address. Make sure they know how to use the graphic organizer to generate ideas for their written responses.

Telephones: Yesterday, Today, and Tomorrow

The telephone is an example of the work of industrial designers. These people make the things we use safer, more useful, and more attractive.

A hundred years ago, a telephone was a box-like thing nailed onto a wall. You had to stand on a chair to reach the call box. You needed to lean forward to speak loudly into the transmitter. You held a small earpiece to your ear to listen. You told the operator a number, and the operator made the connection.

Fifty years later, you could have used the desk phone depicted on the transparency. The design is easier to use because the earpiece and voice transmitter are contained in one piece. You could dial your friend's phone number. When he or she answered, you could speak in a normal voice.

Soon after, there were many phones, designed in all shapes and sizes. The trimline shown in the transparency is small, sleek, and convenient. The dial has been replaced by touch tone, which uses different signals than a dial phone. It is faster and works better.

Fifteen years ago, cordless phones came along. They send radio signals. They do not need attached electric wires. You can wander from room to room, or outside, as you talk.

Today, you might use a cell phone that fits into your pocket easily. Or you might wear a telephone headset which frees your hands to do other things. You may see someone using a cell phone in their car, or while seated in an airplane. Today's phones carry your voice as you move from place to place. Before long, you may own a videophone to make calls. A videophone sends your voice and a TV image of you as well. Designers keep making phones better!

Choose the best answer. Fill in the circle next to your choice.

1. Choose the best summary of this article.

   ○ **A** It explains the purpose of new telephone design.

   ○ **B** It explains why telephones have become smaller and smaller.

   ○ **C** It explains the development of telephone design for the past hundred years and how they may change in the future.

   ○ **D** It explains how phones developed from wired to wireless.

2. The earpiece is the part of the telephone we

   ○ **A** hold to our ear.

   ○ **B** use for dialing.

   ○ **C** hold in our hands.

   ○ **D** install in the wall.

3. According to the article, people no longer use dial phones because touch tone phones

   ○ **A** have better sound.

   ○ **B** are faster and work better.

   ○ **C** can hold ten different phone numbers.

   ○ **D** can hook up to call forwarding.

4. The transmitter is the part of the telephone that

   ○ **A** sends your voice to a receiver.

   ○ **B** replaces the dial on a touch tone phone.

   ○ **C** provides new designs to customers.

   ○ **D** forms the outside covering of the telephone.

5. According to the article, today's industrial designers want to provide

   ○ **A** a telephone that goes with you from place to place.

   ○ **B** a car phone that can call long distance.

   ○ **C** a beeper system that is worldwide.

   ○ **D** telephones on airplanes.

6. The main advantage of a videophone is that it

   ○ **A** provides a way to connect to the World Wide Web.

   ○ **B** can be folded up and put in your pocket.

   ○ **C** can be set up for conference calls.

   ○ **D** allows you to look at the person you are talking to.

Write a Compare and Contrast Paper

Plan and Write Write three paragraphs comparing and contrasting two objects that are the same type but are designed differently. For example, you could compare two bicycles or two clocks. Use the Venn diagram and tips below to help you plan your paragraphs. Write your paragraphs on another sheet of paper.

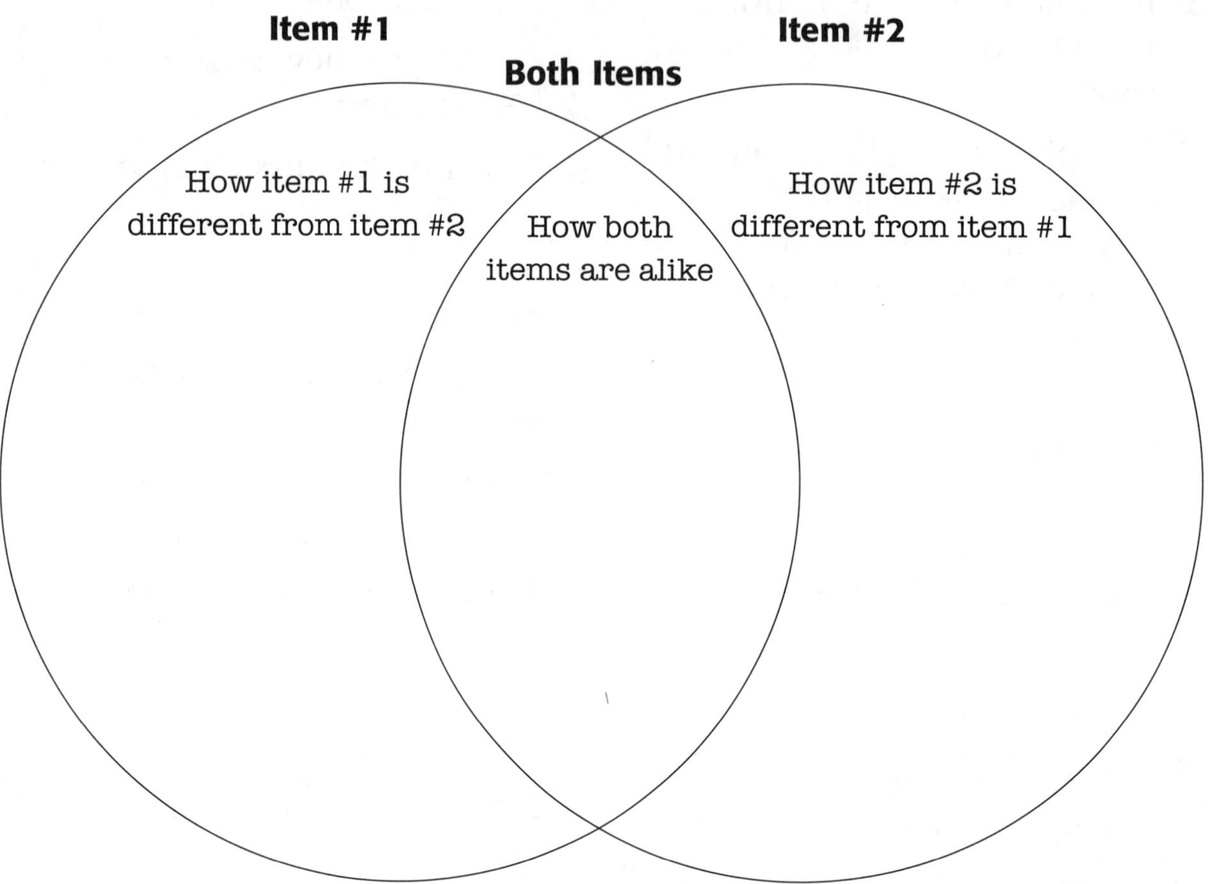

TIPS FOR COMPARING AND CONTRASTING

1. Begin the first paragraph with a topic sentence that tells what you are comparing. Give two or three details that tell how the two items are alike.

2. Begin the second paragraph with a topic sentence, too. Then, give two of three details that tell how the two items are different.

3. Use signal words such as *both* and *neither*.

4. Write a conclusion. Tell why each item's design is good for its purpose.

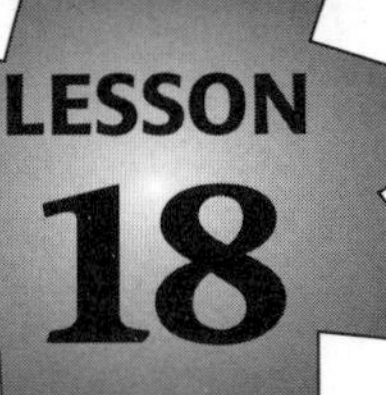

LESSON 18

Why People Wear Masks

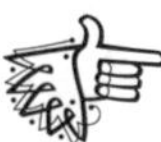 **SET THE STAGE**

Tell students that they will read an article entitled *Why People Wear Masks*. Then, use the Focus on Words section on this page to help them make predictions. You may wish to write the words on the chalkboard.

FOCUS ON WORDS

mosaic   roles

drama   monstrous

ancestor

Make Predictions

RESOURCE:
TRANSPARENCY
3-58

Show the transparency *Mask, Possibly of Tlaloc* (TRANSPARENCY 3-58). Ask: What makes this mask a work of art, not just a mask to wear to a party? Have students think about the words as you read the title of the article. Encourage them to predict how each word could be used in an article that explain, what masks might mean to people of an ancient culture. Use the activity as a springboard to access what they already know about masks. (Possible student response: The mask might be used in a <u>drama</u> to represent a <u>monstrous</u> person.)

Read

Have students read the article on page 118. After they complete the first two paragraphs, pause. Discuss what they have learned so far. Ask students to predict what the rest of the artcle will be about. Then, have them complete the article.

Respond

Help students complete the critical thinking questions on page 119. (See Answer Key, page 127.) Then lead them through the reading of the writing prompt on page 120. Discuss the subject they are to write about, the mode of writing, and the audience they are to address. Make sure they know how to use the graphic organizer to generate ideas for their written responses.

Integrated Reading and Writing: Grade 3

Why People Wear Masks

The Aztec mask in the transparency probably represents an Aztec rain god. The blue stone bits in the mosaic remind us of sky and rain. The face looks powerful and strong. This mask was used in ceremonies about 500 years ago.

People have been making and wearing masks for at l east 30,000 years. Ancient pictures and artworks tell us this. Hunters wore animal masks. Perhaps they felt that their masks would give them the strength and cleverness of the animal. Today, people still feel the mysterious power of masks.

We are easiest to recognize by our faces. When a person puts on a mask, we seem to become another person or being. If you wore the mask shown in the transparency, you would become the spirit represented by the mask. As the spirit, you could do good things for your people, such as bringing good crops. Some cultures made death masks. If you wore the death mask of your ancestor, you were thought to bring the person back to life. Then, the ancestor could tell about the mysteries of death. Masks have also been used to frighten enemies. Warriors sometimes wore monstrous war masks to frighten the people they attacked. It was believed that a scary mask could also chase away demons.

An actor or dancer often puts on a mask to become a character. The first dramas were religious and so were the masks the actors wore. Later, however, actors used masks so they could switch roles easily, and so they could be seen from far away.

We love to put on masks for costume parties or Halloween. Even for an hour, it is fun to have friends and family see us in a new way. Masks have a great power to affect the imagination.

Choose the best answer. Fill in the circle next to your choice.

1. What is one reason NOT given in this article for wearing masks?
   - ○ **A** to seem to become the spirit represented by the mask
   - ○ **B** to bring an ancestor back to life
   - ○ **C** to frighten an enemy
   - ○ **D** to keep people from knowing who you are

2. How long have people been making and wearing masks?
   - ○ **A** about 2,000 years
   - ○ **B** about 50,000 years
   - ○ **C** about 30,000 years
   - ○ **D** about 500 years

3. Which is one reason that actors wore masks?
   - ○ **A** to switch roles easily
   - ○ **B** to frighten the audience
   - ○ **C** to call on the gods for rain
   - ○ **D** to avoid wearing costumes

4. What does the word *monstrous* mean?
   - ○ **A** scary
   - ○ **B** ugly
   - ○ **C** huge
   - ○ **D** dead

5. Which of the following facts was NOT stated in this article?
   - ○ **A** Masks seem to give people a mysterious power.
   - ○ **B** Masks may play a part in a religious activity.
   - ○ **C** Masks can indicate an actor is playing a new part.
   - ○ **D** Masks are valuable if they have valuable jewels attached.

6. What does the word *mosaic* mean in this article?
   - ○ **A** a dancer in a Chinese play
   - ○ **B** a mask worn to frighten animals
   - ○ **C** an artwork made of small colored stones
   - ○ **D** a special mask to call for rain

Write about a Mask

Plan and Write Think of a character you know from a fairy tale or myth. What kind of mask would you design for this character? Write a paragraph for your classmates describing the mask and explaining how it suits the character.

Use the chart below to help you plan your paragraph. Then, write your paragraph on another sheet of paper.

Write a topic sentence naming the character whose mask you are designing.

Topic Sentence:

Describe what the mask will look and feel like.

Looks:
Feels:

Write an ending sentence that sums up the character and the mask you have designed.

Ending Sentence:

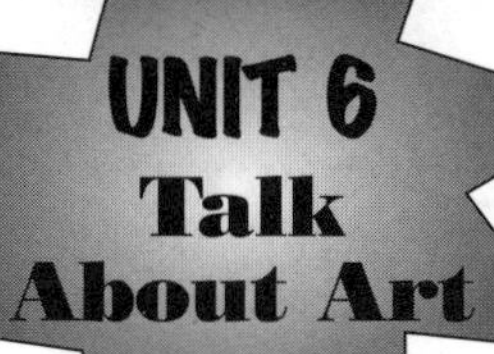

No Written Language

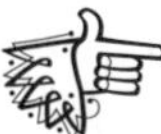

SET THE STAGE

Tell students that they will read an article titled *No Written Language*. Then, use the Focus on Words section on this page to help them make predictions. You may wish to write the words on the chalkboard.

FOCUS ON WORDS

traditions   scripts

benefits   frustrated

Make Predictions

RESOURCE:
TRANSPARENCY
3-50

Show the transparency of Yang Fang Nhu's *Story Cloth* (TRANSPARENCY 3-50). Ask: Do you think a picture story, such as this story cloth, is as effective as a book? Have students think about the words as you read the title of the article. Encourage them to predict how each word could be used in an article about a culture, like the Hmong culture, that has no written language. Use the activity as a springboard to access what they already know about cultures without a written language. (Possible student response: You would not have <u>scripts</u> for TV or movies because these require a written language.)

Read

Have students read the article on page 122. After they complete the first three paragraphs, pause. Discuss what they have learned so far. Ask students to predict what the rest of the article will be about. Then, have them complete the article.

Respond

Help students complete the critical thinking questions on page 123. (See Answer Key, page 127.) Then, lead them through the reading of the writing prompt on page 124. Discuss the subject they are to write about, the mode of writing, and the audience they are to address. Make sure they know how to use the graphic organizer to generate ideas for their written responses.

No Written Language

The Hmong had no written language until about 50 years ago. This means they had no alphabet. They could not read or write because there was no way to shape the sounds into words on a page. They had no books, magazines, or newspapers. But stories and art, like the story cloth, were handed down from parents to children. This was their way of keeping their traditions and history alive.

Imagine what your life would be like without the benefits of a written language! At breakfast, there would be no cereal boxes with words on them. None of your food would be in packages printed with information. In fact, nothing you used every day would tell you anything.

When you left home, there would be no signs on streets or stores to guide you. If you stopped to buy lunch, there would be no menu. Whenever you wanted something, you would be frustrated because you would need to wait and ask for it.

There would be no school—at least not the way you know it. You would get a job and adults would show you how to do work. They would pass along stories that had been told to them. There would be no TV when you got home from work. Actors need written scripts. Reporters rely on the printed word to give you news. What is more, people need books that train them to operate TV equipment. Computers, movies, and advertisements would also be missing.

A society without a written language is simple and slow. Our culture moves very quickly because it is run by information based on written language. Computers and machines have made our culture even speedier. Without writing, you would live a much different life than you do. How would you like it?

Choose the best answer. Fill in the circle next to your choice.

1. Approximately when did the Hmong acquire a written language?

   ○ **A** 1950

   ○ **B** 1925

   ○ **C** 1975

   ○ **D** 1910

2. Which of the following would we NOT have without a written language?

   ○ **A** wildflowers

   ○ **B** artworks

   ○ **C** movies and TV shows

   ○ **D** ocean breezes

3. According to the article, how did the Hmong preserve their history?

   ○ **A** through stories told from mother to daughter

   ○ **B** through artworks, like the story cloth

   ○ **C** through tape recordings

   ○ **D** by memorizing their history

4. How would our lives change if we had no written language?

   ○ **A** There would be more attention paid to art.

   ○ **B** Our lives would move more quickly.

   ○ **C** Our lives would move more slowly.

   ○ **D** There would be more interest in money.

5. The word *benefits* in this article means

   ○ **A** important things.

   ○ **B** good things.

   ○ **C** needs.

   ○ **D** fears.

6. What does the word *scripts* mean in this article?

   ○ **A** a memory course for people

   ○ **B** pages written for the actors in a play

   ○ **C** part of the set of a drama

   ○ **D** supports for a stage

Name____ Date____________ Class____________

Write a Fantasy Story

Plan and Write What if you awoke one day and found you couldn't understand a word of the language in your world? Write a fantasy for your teacher about what happens as you try to get through the day. Use the story map below to plan your story. Then, write your story on another sheet of paper.

Name your characters, including yourself. Tell where and when the story takes place. Write a beginning sentence that grabs your readers, attention.

Characters:	Where:
	When:

What problem do the characters have? Tell about it in a sentence.

Problem:

Tell what happens to the characters and what they do.

First Event:

Second Event:

Third Event:

How does the story end? Tell how the problem is solved.

Solution:

Answer Key

UNIT 1

Opener, Answers for page 7
1. A how a painting looks from two different distances
2. C view very small things
3. B living things.
4. D They both show details.
5. B they want to see the universe clearly.
6. A to show details of the moon over the park.

Lesson 1, Answers for page 11
1. B United States holiday.
2. D at first.
3. A brings different ideas to our minds.
4. B write letters to authors
5. A They both celebrate a time in history.
6. C Holidays Around the World.

Lesson 2, Answers for page 15
1. B Playing Games of Make-Believe
2. A of special importance.
3. C enjoy games of all kinds.
4. D games people still play today.
5. A All of us love to play games.
6. C the player will catch the ball.

Lesson 3, Answers for page 18
1. C something you want to touch.
2. B Wilbur.
3. A a warm and obedient pet.
4. D thinks better.
5. D the reputation of pigs.
6. C they all have qualities we admire.

Write About Art, Answers for page 23
1. D She has a great imagination.
2. B a destination you want to reach
3. D They both show paths from one place to another.
4. A The picture looks like both a maze and a map.
5. B Lena's Unusual Journeys
6. A a picture that is a maze and a map

UNIT 2

Opener, Answers for page 27
1. C An Artist Paints His Dreams
2. D Some people think this is Chagall's most beautiful painting.
3. A happiness.
4. D a hunter.
5. C unusual.
6. D he is showing his memories and his dreams.

Lesson 4, Answers for page 31
1. B Cool colors help patients relax.
2. C colors
3. A blended these colors with related colors
4. D Real tree trunks contain shades of browns, blacks, and grays.
5. D life itself.
6. B an outdoor scene

Lesson 5, Answers for page 35
1. C gratitude
2. A a bowl of fruit
3. D Paying Tribute to People We Admire
4. C position.
5. B to imitate them.
6. C to honor great artists of the past

Lesson 6, Answers for page 39
1. C Where the Inuit live, winter usually lasts ten months.
2. A stories
3. B to honor the spirits of game animals
4. B A young owl is taking a piggyback ride with its mother.
5. D walruses.
6. C a holy man

Artist at Work, Answers for page 43
1. D the artist and his wife
2. C line
3. C hundreds of years
4. C to protect the person
5. A hundreds of years ago
6. B to protect

UNIT 3

Opener, Answers for page 47
1. A   form.
2. C   Louise Nevelson made her sculpture from found objects.
3. D   purity.
4. B   structure.
5. C   about two thousand years
6. B   the ring

Lesson 7, Answers for page 51
1. C   a cone
2. B   a place to live
3. A   set poles in a circle in the ground
4. C   They were a wandering people.
5. B   It forms an attic where children can sleep.
6. A   a ball

Lesson 8, Answers for page 55
1. C   that his puppet would become a real boy
2. A   His nose grew.
3. B   happy
4. D   a troublemaker
5. D   He goes to Pleasure Island.
6. A   bad luck

Lesson 9, Answers for page 59
1. B   a single person.
2. C   silent
3. D   three lifelike statues
4. D   Mime is an art form that is performed in silence.
5. A   interior.
6. C   quiet

Talk About Art, Answers for page 63
1. A   the arrangement of the parts.
2. B   The snake grew too big for its skin and shed it.
3. D   found objects
4. A   early in the day
5. B   a tree branch
6. C   there are many different things to look at.

UNIT 4

Opener, Answers for page 67
1. A   During the Renaissance, silks and velvets were popular fabrics.
2. C   jewels
3. D   They wear hoops underneath their clothing.
4. B   designed to show the shape of the body.
5. B   they wanted to look as perfect as possible.
6. D   a hoop

Lesson 10, Answers for page 71
1. C   Rosie had fifteen puppies.
2. B   to help Rosie feed the puppies
3. C   several weeks
4. A   well-rounded
5. C   by eating their way across the pan
6. A   twisting and turning

Lesson 11, Answers for page 75
1. C   people who wander in search of food
2. B   They did not know how to farm.
3. A   People had the leisure time to think.
4. C   grains
5. A   Thanksgiving Day.
6. C   a grain

Lesson 12, Answers for page 79
1. A   to keep grave robbers out
2. A   The sides of the pyramid go up in steps.
3. B   a temple
4. B   builder.
5. C   They were centers for Mayan worship.
6. B   four sides.

Talk About Art, Answers for page 83
1. A   staying alive.
2. B   They have more energy.
3. B   a plan.
4. C   warriors.
5. C   games that require mental strength
6. D   Laughter is the best medicine.

UNIT 5

Opener, Answers for page 87
1. C   A home expresses a family's thoughts and feelings.
2. C   a religious statue.
3. B   They enjoy animals.
4. D   a statue in the yard
5. A   displaying a wreath
6. B   a small part.

Lesson 13, Answers for page 91
1. A   blanket.
2. D   squares and triangles and other shapes.
3. C   A quilt could tell what a woman believed in.
4. B   They may use computer-made designs.
5. A   people of the community.
6. C   history.

Lesson 14, Answers for page 95
1. B   a posed photograph of a person
2. A   A good photograph can show someone's inner personality.
3. C   without the subject knowing it.
4. D   planned.
5. A   Certain objects can show what a person likes to do.
6. C   Photographs have a certain magic.

Lesson 15, Answers for page 99
1. B   The computer helps industrial designers learn more and work faster.
2. B   produced.
3. A   to find out what will happen when someone walks in the shoe
4. B   exact.
5. D   They made drawings by hand.
6. C   which stores will sell the new toy

Talk About Art, Answers for page 103
1. C   make pure.
2. B   not easily changed.
3. C   to advertise.
4. D   It brightens the neon.
5. A   early in the century
6. A   They add other gases to it.

UNIT 6

Opener, Answers for page 107
1. A   to remember the past
2. C   a chance.
3. B   if the language in the new country is different
4. A   leaves his or her native land.
5. B   the songs, dances, or food from the old country
6. D   the land where you were born

Lesson 16, Answers for page 111
1. C   a child about your age
2. B   a blue cloth with green plants and fish and rocks in other colors
3. B   after they beat the cloth with sticks
4. D   sticky starch.
5. B   after the wax was put on it
6. A   something used to color cloth

Lesson 17, Answers for page 115
1. C   It tracks the development of telephone design for the past hundred years.
2. A   hold to our ear.
3. B   are faster and work better.
4. A   sends your voice to a receiver.
5. A   a telephone that goes with you from place to place.
6. D   allows you to look at the person you are talking to.

Lesson 18, Answers for page 119
1. D   to keep people from knowing who you are
2. C   about 30,000 years
3. A   to switch roles easily
4. A   scary
5. D   Masks are valuable if they have valuable jewels attached.
6. C   an artwork made of small colored stones

Talk About Art, Answers for page 123
1. A   1950
2. C   movies and TV shows
3. B   through artworks, like the story cloth
4. C   Our lives would move more slowly.
5. B   good things.
6. B   pages written for the actors in a play

Word Webs

Before students read an article, you might ask them to make word webs. This exercise will help them develop vocabulary and will tap into what they already know about the subject.

Example: A word web may have a vocabulary word or a concept at its center. Students brainstorm other words to add around the sides.

The title of the lesson *A Wedding Sculpture* suggests that the concept wedding is central to the article. Place the word in the center of the web. Ask students to brainstorm words that they may encounter in the article. The final product might look like this:

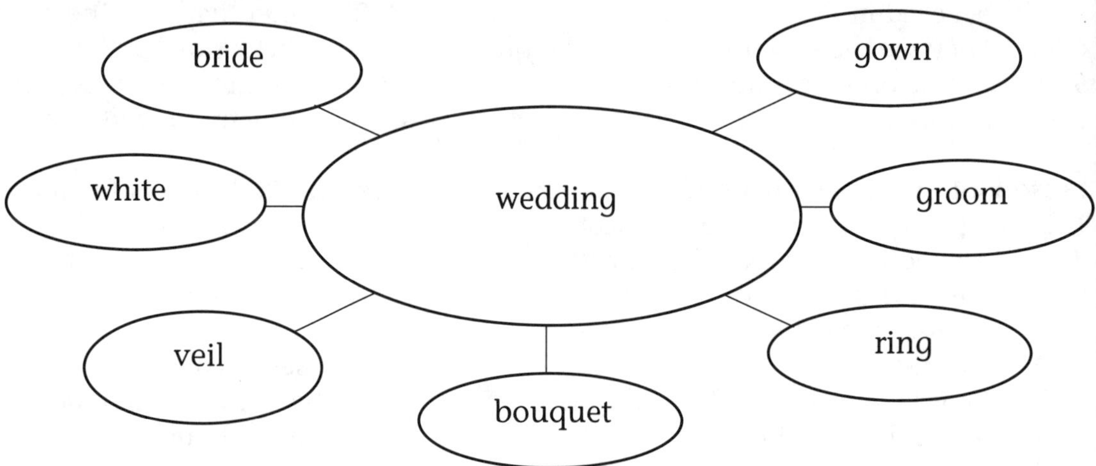

Prediction Chart

Vocabulary words pre-selected for an article can also serve to help students make predictions. Ask students to choose a word that seems to suggest something about the article. Have them write it down on the prediction chart. Then, ask students to jot down any prediction it suggests.

Example: The Focus on Words section for the lesson *What Quilts Express* contains the word *geometric*. Place the word on the chart. Ask students to use the word to make predictions. The final product might look like this:

Clue Word	Prediction
geometric	The article may tell about how to make a quilt because quilts are made of pieces of cloth that have geometric shapes, like squares and triangles.

Word Web

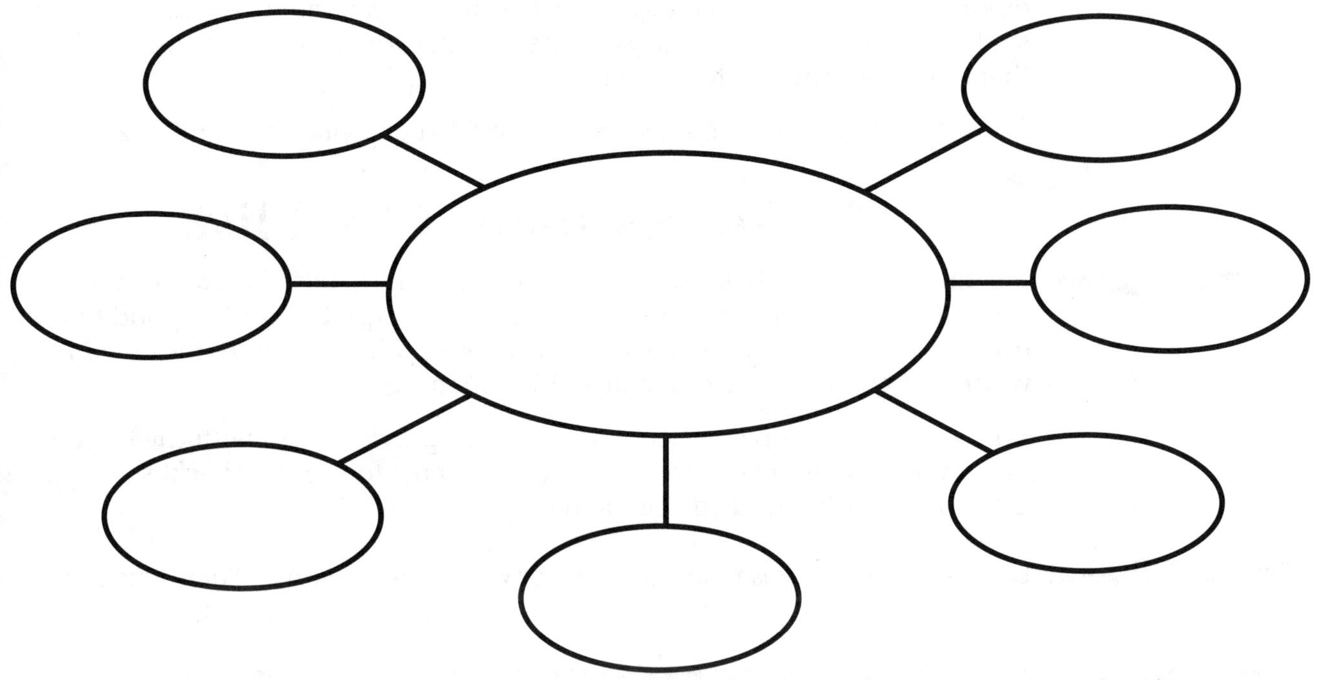

Prediction Chart

Clue Word	Prediction

Graphic Organizers

A graphic organizer is provided with each writing prompt. The graphic organizer guides students through necessary pre-writing activites. Encourage students to use these organizers as they think through their responses. Have them jot down their notes in the spaces provided.

Two additional blackline masters are provided on pages 131 and 132.

Self-Assessment Checklists

Writing Sample The final activity in each lesson is a writing activity based on a writing prompt. The students must read the prompt, interpret it, and respond to it in a written composition. This activity will help students prepare for the kind of writing assessments used in state achievement tests.

When students complete their compositions, provide them with the appropriate self-assessment checklist. Encourage students to use the checklists to guide their proofreading and editing activities.

Types of Writing Each prompt requires a specific type of writing in response. Each type has a specific subject, a specific mode, and a specific audience as follows:

Type of Writing	Student Response
Informative/Descriptive	The student will use facts to convey information. The student will describe features and qualities of an idea or of an object.
Narrative	The student will tell a story, using chronological order to keep events in order.
Expressive/Narrative	The student will express his or her own thoughts or feelings. The student will write in sequential order, as dictated by the prompt.
Informative/Classificatory	The student will use facts to convey information. The student will group elements based on their characteristics.
Persuasive	The student will use reasons to support a point of view and try to persuade an audience. The student will describe features and qualities of an idea or of an object for the purpose of persuading their audience.

Venn Diagram

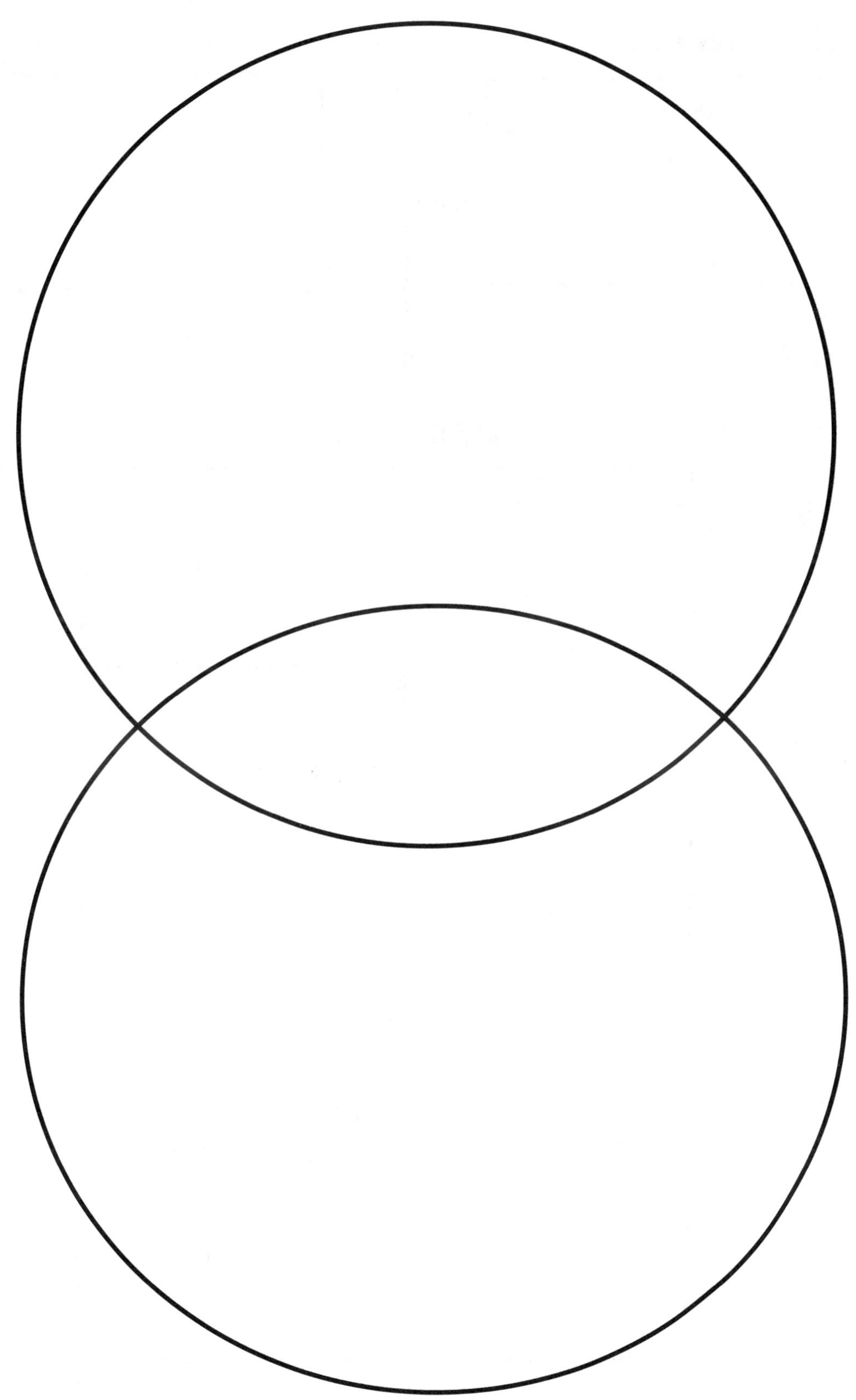

Story Map

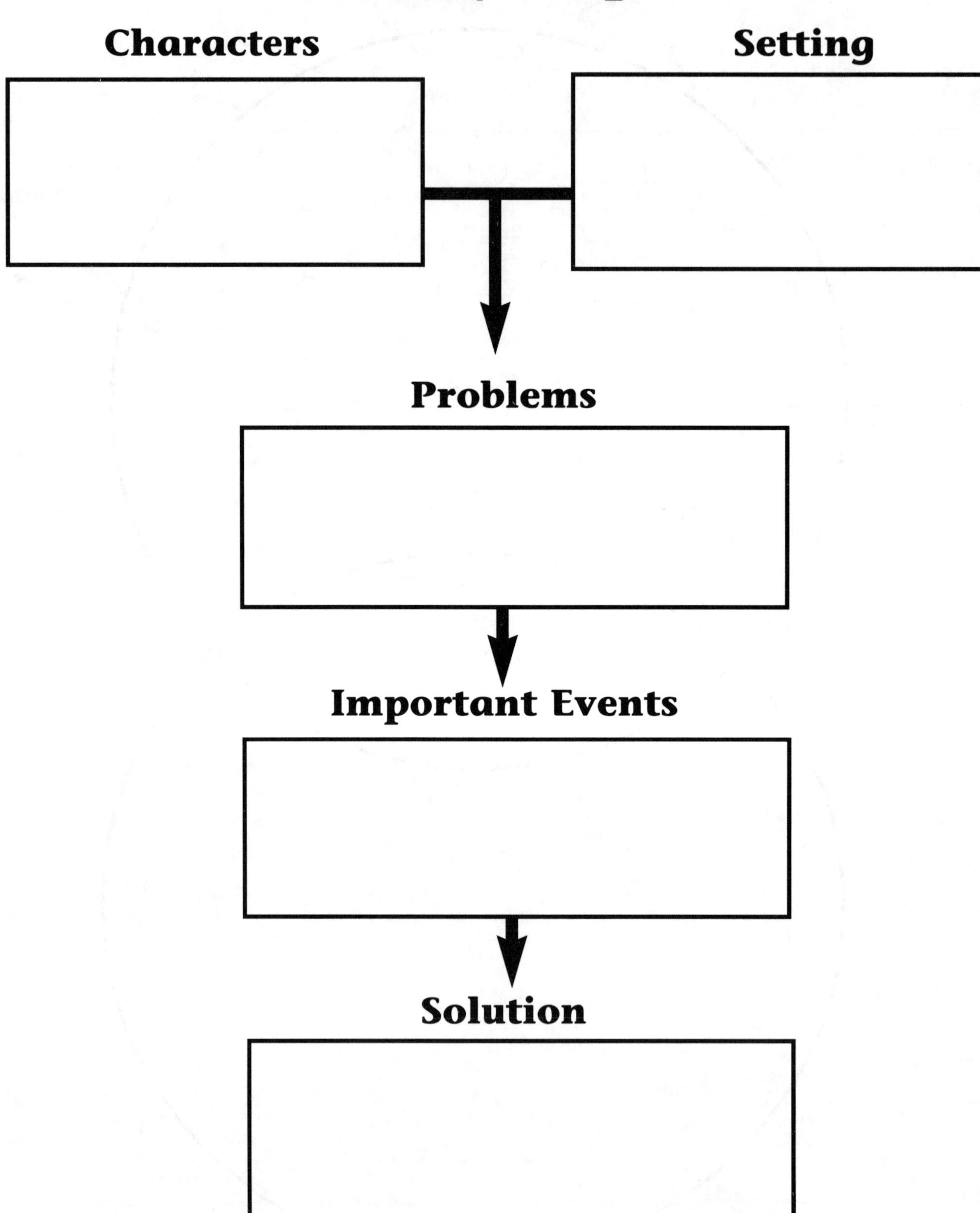

Name____

Read each question below. Choose the answer that best reflects your description. Check one of the boxes on the right.

Title of Work ____________________________ ____________________________	🙂 **Yes!** I did this well.	☹ **No!** I need to work on this.
Did I write what the writing prompt said to write?		
Is my description well organized?		
Is my description clear and complete?		
Do I have details that appeal to the senses?		
Do I have a topic sentence?		
Do I keep to the topic throughout?		
Will my description appeal to my audience?		
Do I use interesting words and phrases?		
Do I have a variety of sentence types and lengths?		

✔ Self-Assessment Checklist: Informative Writing

Read each question below. Choose the answer that best reflects your
information. Check one of the boxes on the right.

Title of Work __________________________________ ___________________________________	☺ **Yes!** I did this well.	☹ **No!** I need to work on this.
Did I write what the writing prompt said to write?		
Have I given the information in an organized way?		
Is the information clear and complete?		
Do I have details or examples?		
Do I have a topic sentence?		
Do I keep to the topic throughout?		
Will my composition appeal to my audience?		
Do I use interesting words and phrases?		
Do I have a variety of sentence types and lengths?		
Have I proofread for correct spelling and grammar?		

✔ Self-Assessment Checklist: Narrative Writing

Read each question below. Choose the answer that best reflects your
narrative. Check one of the boxes on the right.

Title of Work ________________________ ________________________	☺ **Yes!** I did this well.	☹ **No!** I need to work on this.
Did I write what the writing prompt said to write?		
Does my story have a setting?		
Do I have interesting characters?		
Do I start off with some kind of a problem?		
Do I tell the events in sequential order?		
Do I solve the problem at the end?		
Will my story appeal to my audience?		
Do I use interesting words and phrases?		
Do I have a variety of sentence types and lengths?		

✔ Self-Assessment Checklist: Persuasive Writing

Read each question below. Choose the answer that best reflects your persuasive writing. Check one of the boxes on the right.

Title of Work ________________________ ________________________	:) **Yes!** I did this well.	:(**No!** I need to work on this.
Did I write what the writing prompt said to write?		
Do I present an opinion on the topic?		
Do I give reasons to support my opinion?		
Do I give details and examples?		
Do I have a topic sentence?		
Do I keep to the topic throughout?		
Will my composition appeal to my audience?		
Do I use interesting words and phrases?		
Do I have a variety of sentence types and lengths?		

✔ Self-Assessment Checklist: Proofreading

Read each question below. Choose the answer that best reflects your description. Check one of the boxes on the right.

Title of Work ________________________ ________________________	😊 **Yes!** I did this well.	☹ **No!** I need to work on this.
Do the parts of each sentence agree?		
Have I avoided sentence fragments?		
Have I avoided run-on sentences?		
Have I used capital letters correctly?		
Have I used punctuation marks correctly?		
Is each word spelled correctly?		
Is my handwriting neat and readable?		

     WRITING STRATEGIES: PROOFREADING   137

Art-Related Words Lessons in *Integrated Reading and Writing* introduce and review art-related words already taught in the *Portfolios* program for this grade level.

The following pages (pp.138-144) contain these words on blackline masters in the form of word cards. Each word card is identified by the unit and lesson where you will find it in *Integrated Reading and Writing.*

Templates for blank cards that you and your students can use are also available. Students can use these to make word cards of their own.

Suggestions for Using the Word Cards

Review Use the word cards as a springboard for reviewing unit concepts. Place the word cards for the unit (or units) you are reviewing in a box. Ask a student to choose a card. The student must then either explain the meaning of the word or create an example of it.

Word Banks Ask students to add the word cards to already existing word banks for reading and language arts. Ask students to use the words whenever they undertake a writing assignment.

Word Sorts Ask students to sort the words according to categories: color words; computer words; and math words for example. You may wish to have students make up their own categories: words for things that glow; things that take up space; things or ideas that we cannot see (abstract words).

Apply Word Cards to Everyday Art Ask students to create a bulletin board or display of everyday art. For example, students can leaf through old magazines to pick out pictures or advertisements that they feel have artistic merit. They can also bring in products (perfume bottles, a can of food, for example) that have an artistic flair. Students can then "label" their pieces with a Word Card to point out the merit of their chosen piece. Allow plenty of class time for discussion of the artworks and the labels.

Test Review Before tests, pair up students. Make sure each student has a set of word cards. Ask students to review the art vocabulary by using the word cards in various kinds of guessing games and card games.

Word Cards

universal Unit 1, Lesson 1	gallery Unit 1, Opener
center of interest Unit 1, Lesson 2	microscope Unit 1, Opener
motion Unit 1, Lesson 2	organisms Unit 1, Opener
expression Unit 1, Lesson 3	telescope Unit 1, Opener
outwits Unit 1, Lesson 3	international Unit 1, Lesson 1
talents Unit 1, Lesson 3	significance Unit 1, Lesson 1

Word Cards

texture	primary colors
Unit 1, Lesson 3	Unit 2, Opener
challenge	color scheme
Unit 1, Write About Art	Unit 2, Lesson 4
destination	cool colors
Unit 1, Write About Art	Unit 2, Lesson 4
goal	hues
Unit 1, Write About Art	Unit 2, Lesson 4
images	related colors
Unit 2, Opener	Unit 2, Lesson 4
overlap	warm colors
Unit 2, Opener	Unit 2, Lesson 4

Word Cards

pose — Unit 2, Lesson 5	shaman — Unit 2, Lesson 6
rectangles — Unit 2, Lesson 5	shield — Unit 2, Artist at Work
still life — Unit 2, Lesson 5	slanted line — Unit 2, Artist at Work
masks — Unit 2, Lesson 6	assemblage — Unit 3, Opener
myths — Unit 2, Lesson 6	found object — Unit 3, Opener
print — Unit 2, Lesson 6	sculpture — Unit 3, Opener

Word Cards

asymetrical balance

Unit 3, Lesson 8

puppet

Unit 3, Lesson 8

exterior

Unit 3, Lesson 9

subject

Unit 3, Lesson 9

vertical lines

Unit 3, Lesson 9

balance

Unit 3, Talk About Art

symbol

Unit 3, Opener

cone

Unit 3, Lesson 7

cube

Unit 3, Lesson 7

cylinder

Unit 3, Lesson 7

pyramid

Unit 3, Lesson 7

sphere

Unit 3, Lesson 7

Word Cards

squirmy

Unit 4, Lesson 10

agriculture

Unit 4, Lesson 11

legumes

Unit 4, Lesson 11

nomads

Unit 4, Lesson 11

architect

Unit 4, Lesson 12

jeweled

Unit 4, Lesson 12

variety

Unit 3, Talk About Art

farthingale

Unit 4, Opener

contrast

Unit 4, Opener

gems

Unit 4, Opener

blended

Unit 4, Lesson 10

plump

Unit 4, Lesson 10

Word Cards

shrine
Unit 5, Opener

sculpture
Unit 5, Opener

geometric
Unit 5, Lesson 13

quilts
Unit 5, Lesson 13

traditional
Unit 5, Lesson 13

visual rhythm
Unit 5, Lesson 13

monument
Unit 4, Lesson 12

rectangle
Unit 4, Lesson 12

accomplish
Unit 4, About Art

culture
Unit 4, About Art

survival
Unit 4, About Art

detail
Unit 5, Opener

Word Cards

models Unit 5, Lesson 15	candid Unit 5, Lesson 14
electrons Unit 5, Talk About Art	composed Unit 5, Lesson 14
neon Unit 5, Talk About Art	photographs Unit 5, Lesson 14
emigrant Unit 6, Opener	portraits Unit 5, Lesson 14
native land Unit 6, Opener	CAD–Computer Aided Design Unit 5, Lesson 15
opportunity Unit 6, Opener	manufactured Unit 5, Lesson 15

Word Cards

batik Unit 6, Lesson 16	sleek Unit 6, Lesson 17
dye Unit 6, Lesson 16	transmitter Unit 6, Lesson 17
glazes Unit 6, Lesson 16	ancestor Unit 6, Lesson 18
sizing Unit 6, Lesson 16	drama Unit 6, Lesson 18
tjanting Unit 6, Lesson 16	monstrous Unit 6, Lesson 18
headset Unit 6, Lesson 17	mosaic Unit 6, Lesson 18

roles

Unit 6, Lesson 18

scripts

Unit 6, Talk About Art

Word Cards

Word Cards

Word Cards

Word Cards

Word Cards